The Twelve Steps of Phobics Anonymous

Rosemary and Marilyn

The Twelve Steps of Phobics Anonymous was officially introduced at the 10th National Conference on Phobias and Related Anxiety Disorders, Sponsored by the Phobia Society of America, now the Anxiety Disorder Association of America which was held March 1990 in Washington D.C. United States of America.

ISBN 978-0-9972085-7-3 (paperback)
ISBN 978-0-9972085-6-6 (ebook)

Library of Congress Control Number: 2016960284

Published by AquaZebra, www.AquaZebra.com

AquaZebra™
Book Publishing

Author: Rosemary

Book Designer Mark E. Anderson, AquaZebra

AquaZebra™
Web, Book & Print Design
www.AquaZebra.com

Lance Gerber - Original Phobics Anonymous Logo Artist

The Twelve Steps of Alcoholics Anonymous
Printed and Adapted with Permission of AA World Services, Inc.

Printed in the United States of America.

Table of Contents

Our Symbol

<u>THE EIGHT-SIDED OCTAGON</u> is recognized as the universal stop sign. We in Phobics Anonymous chose this symbol to serve as a constant reminder that we must <u>STOP</u> catastrophic, negative, fearful thought processes and behaviors. We must <u>STOP</u> blaming people, places and things for our problems and begin looking at our own reflection in the mirror.

<u>THE BUTTERFLY</u> at the top of the octagon symbolizes the freedom we experience upon working the 12 steps of Phobics Anonymous. It is the most human of all insects for the pain of its metamorphosis most closely resembles the pain experienced in human growth. The struggles which the Butterfly undergoes to emerge from its chrysalis, is what gives the Butterfly the strength to live.

<u>THE INITIALS "P""A"</u> of Phobics Anonymous also serve as a devastating reminder of Panic Attacks which gave birth to the fellowship of Phobics Anonymous.

<u>THE SOLID DOUBLE LINE</u> around the octagon symbolizes the fact that we cannot do it alone. When we change the "me" to "we", we gain a sense of connection with others which helps build the spiritual foundation and enables us, with the help of our Higher Power, to gain strength, become healthy, whole, and free.

Proclamation
City of Palm Springs
CALIFORNIA

WHEREAS, Palm Springs is now the World Service Headquarters of Phobics Anonymous, adapting the 12-step approach to the treatment of panic and anxiety disorders; and

WHEREAS, According to the National Institute of Mental Health and The Phobia Society of America, anxiety and panic related disorders are the number one mental health problem in the world today; and

WHEREAS, For millions of people chronic worry, psychological stress, acute anxiety, and overwhelming panic are constant companions, invading all aspects of their lives; and

WHEREAS, For one in five individuals irrational fears are equal opportunity afflictions, crossing all barriers of race, religion and creed; and

WHEREAS, A large number of those afflicted develop concurrent problems such as alcohol or drug abuse, in a desperate effort to cope with the anxiety;

NOW, THEREFORE, I, SONNY BONO, Mayor of the City of Palm Springs, California, do hereby proclaim the month of March 1990

ANXIETY AND PHOBIC AWARENESS MONTH

in our beautiful City and I urge all citizens to join me in commending The Institute for Phobic Awareness and its founder Marilyn Gellis for efforts in the identification of and rehabilitation of afflicted persons.

Dated this 6th Day of February, 1990

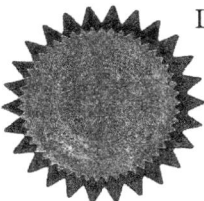

Sonny Bono

_____

Mayor

Dedication

This book is dedicated to the loving memory of my mother, Jean Gellis, who died December 24, 1989, still not able to understand why her "beautiful, intelligent, gifted" daughter, her "pride and joy" who travelled around the world by herself, worked her way through college and graduate school, relocated in California with only fifty dollars in her pocket, produced, directed and starred in her own educational T.V. program; wrote ten motivational math books, served as a math consultant and lectured in front of thousands of people all over the United States,

ONE DAY WAS

Unable to shop in a market and fled in terror, leaving the shopping cart at the check-out stand;

Could not sit next to her in temple, because she liked front and center, and I had to sit in the back row on the aisle;

Was unable to drive her to visit her friends or pick her up at the airport when she flew out for a vacation because driving caused acute panic attacks;

Turned down invitation after invitation and refused to go to a restaurant, movie, party, or any other social function;

And finally reached the point where I didn't answer my telephone, couldn't leave my house and spent my days and nights crying...

Introduction

"Humans always ... fear an unknown situation. This is normal. The important thing is what we do about it: If fear is permitted to become a paralyzing thing that interferes with proper action, then it is harmful. The best antidote to fear is to know all we can about a situation."

- John H. Glenn, Jr.

For many people, chronic worry, psychological stress, self-defeating fears, acute anxiety, and overwhelming panic are constant unseen yet powerful companions doggedly following each and every step we take, cutting into life and squeezing the joy out of living. Daily normal routines are no longer fulfilling for some, lack luster for most, and become impossible for others.

FEAR is the Four-letter word which touches every aspect of our lives - an evil and corroding thread woven through the fabric of our existence. It is not the private domain of the weak. It strikes the mighty and powerful as well, enslaving us by making us prisoners. Condemned by our catastrophic negative thoughts, we become physically, emotionally, and spiritually bankrupt. We give it the power to slap handcuffs and shackles on our lives. Many of us become victims of frustration, despair, depression or hopelessness, and sometimes suicidal. Our perspective of life becomes warped. Like a virus which begins with one fearful experience or situation, it spreads and infects all other areas of our lives which, in themselves, are completely removed from any damage that can act as a trigger.

The biggest casualty of fear is loss of intimacy with a Higher Power. FEAR is The OPPOSITE of FAITH! The two cannot co-exist in the same place at the same time. In order to aid our recovery we must live by faith and not by sight.

"For those who believe, no proof is necessary - for those who don't believe, no proof is possible."

Nothing is more satisfying and encouraging in our relationship with our Higher Power than to be able to "offer things up", - let them go and then to relax, and watch the spiritual intervention in our difficulties.

Let Go and Let God

> *As children bring their broken toys*
> *with tears for us to mend I brought my*
> *broken dreams to God because he was my*
> *friend -*
> *But then instead of leaving him in peace to*
> *work alone I hung around and tried to help*
> *with ways that were my own.*
> *At last, I snatched them back and cried,*
> *"How could you be so slow?"*
> *"My child," He said, "What could I do?*
>
> *You never did let go ..."*

Circumstances get altered and outcomes get adjusted. We then find that we have the inner direction and strength to stand and face our fears rather than retreat.

According to the National Institute of Mental Health, anxiety and panic disorders are the number one mental health problem in the United States today. They affect a minimum of 10% of the population at any given time. Yet a recent scientific study shows that patients with anxiety disorders and major depressions contain the lowest percentage of believers in a Higher Power. They were also the least spiritually oriented group.

Psychiatry, one of the most popular methods of therapy, for all practical purposes, has generally excluded the spiritual factor of recovery and, although this aspect has been largely ignored by other forms of therapy as well, we of Phobics Anonymous find it a vital component to our recovery process.

We must make it clear that there is a difference between spirituality and religion. A **Higher Power** is **not** to be confused with a church, temple, or any religious denomination.

Our Twelve Step Program is in no way religious in the sense of dogma, doctrines, codes, or beliefs. Although we do incorporate and make use of the basic principles of all of the major world religions, we are not a religious organization, or cult. We are not affiliated with any single denomination.

We have found in working with phobics there must be a joining of resources. Just as a chair or table has four legs to be balanced - so it is with our lives. The intellectual, physical, emotional, and spiritual aspects are all related and relevant. All must be addressed and given equal value.

Many of you who read this may balk at the idea of a Higher Power, so please, before you tune us out, read on. To those who have no acquaintance, the existence of a "Higher Power", may appear to be a rash claim, but it needs only a willingness and a fair trial. You've probably tried everything else and run the gambit from psychiatrists, psychologists, counselors, doctors, etc., ad nauseam, to no avail, so why not give this a chance. What have you got to lose except your problem?

The Higher Power Concept

> I believe in the sun even when it is not shining.
> I believe in love even when not feeling it.
> I believe in a Higher Power even when it is silent.

Our Higher Power does not need a name attached to it such as "God". Our conception, however inadequate, is sufficient to make the approach and effect a contact. Many of us were, and still are suspicious and skeptical because of disappointments we experienced with organized religions. Some of us are agnostics and atheists, but still there is a spirit or an energy that can be felt at our Twelve-Step meetings. We are a fellowship and all of our members are free to choose the concept of a Higher Power that works best for them.

For some, the concept of a Higher Power can be the power of the program. For others, a Higher Power represents the goodness, caring, compassion, and support of the group they are attending. For some, a force or creative intelligence; for others, some aspect of nature or a spirit of the universe.

When you can answer "yes" to the question, "Do I now, or can I ever believe there is a power greater than myself?", you are well on your way toward working the Twelve Steps.

This book is meant to be suggestive only. It is not intended to substitute for nor replace medical care and/or supervision. It in no way is intended to conflict with any form of treatment or therapy which has been proven successful for you in the past. We do not take issue with, nor do we disregard health measures. We strongly feel that some services and medications are indispensable in the treatment of anxiety and panic-related disorders. We also strongly recommend that a complete physical exam be taken before embarking on any program to eliminate any existing health problems which might be causing panic-related symptoms.

"The largest room in the world is the room for improvement."

1

Who, What and Why of Phobics Anonymous

"We are largely the playthings of our fears.

In one, fear of the dark;

to another, of physical pain;

to a third, of public ridicule;

to a fourth, of poverty;

to a fifth, of loneliness;

for all of us,

our particular creature waits in ambush."

- Horace Walpole
British Author

Who is a Phobic?

We are a group of individuals who found that we are powerless over fear. We experience irrational fears often accompanied by acute anxiety and panic attacks. At times, we experienced the following physical symptoms to such an extent that they made our lives unmanageable.

The Anxiety Scale

Functional

1. "Butterflies", a queasy feeling in stomach, trembling, jitteriness, tension.

2. Cold or clammy palms, hot flashes and warm all over, profuse sweating.

3. Very rapid, strong, racing, pounding or irregular heartbeat, tremors, muscle tension and aches, fatigue.

Decreased Functional Ability

4. Jelly legs, wobbly, weak in knees, unsteady feelings, shakiness.

5. Immediate desperate and urgent need to escape, avoid or hide.

6. Lump in throat, dry mouth, choking, muscle tension.

7. Hyperventilation, tightness in chest, shortness of breath, smothering sensation.

Very Limited or Completely Non-Functional

8. Feelings of impending doom or death, high pulse rate, difficulty breathing, palpitations.

9. Dizziness, visual distortion, faintness, headache, nausea, numbness, tingling of hands, feet or other body parts, diarrhea, frequent urination.

10. COMPLETE PANIC, non-functional, disoriented, detached, feelings of unreality, paralyzed, fear of dying, going crazy, or losing control.*

*Frequently people experiencing their first spontaneous "panic attack", rush to emergency rooms convinced that they are having a heart attack.

Our fear of being trapped in our emotions, made us feel we were either going crazy, going to lose control, or die. The perimeter of our world became smaller and smaller as we avoided situations, people, and places; such as markets, restaurants, theaters, social functions, driving, job related activities, etc.

We sought help from physicians, psychologists, psychiatrists, hypnotherapists, nutritionists, family, and friends. Many of us self-medicated with alcohol and drugs. All of these provided temporary relief. They addressed the physical, emotional, and intellectual part of man. Yet, there was a missing link. We found the recovery process was incomplete without addressing the spiritual aspect of man.

What is the Phobics Anonymous Program?

Phobics Anonymous is a society of men and women for whom fear, anxiety and panic attacks have become a major problem and a controlling entity within their lives.

Through the years, we found fear to be an equal opportunity affliction crossing all barriers of age, race, religion, and creed. Our program consists of a set of principles so basic, uncomplicated, and simple that we can incorporate them in our daily living. Documented experience in other twelve step fellowships like Alcoholics Anonymous or Narcotics Anonymous prove that these principles work. We have learned from our own personal experience that those who faithfully work the program, continue to attend meetings, and read The Twelve Steps of Phobics Anonymous literature, experience success in the recovery process.

Why is Phobics Anonymous here?

When the quality of our lives became so devastated, desperate, and hopeless, we sought help. We had become prisoners of our fears. We were in bondage. We became afraid to live and afraid to die. Our self-defeating fears had become a near fatal disease or illness that dictated our actions, shrunk our world, and ruled our lives. We came to Phobics Anonymous in search of help and freedom. We realized then that we were not alone. We had found a "safe place".

How does Phobics Anonymous work?

If you want what we have to offer and are willing to make any effort, then you are ready to take certain steps. These are the principles that aided us in our recovery process.

The Twelve Steps of Phobics Anonymous

1. We admitted that we were powerless over Fear - that our lives had become unmanageable.

2. Came to believe that a power greater than ourselves could restore us to wholeness.

3. Made a decision to turn our will and our lives over to the care of God, as we understood Him.

4. Made a searching and fearless moral inventory of ourselves.

5. Admitted to our God, to ourselves, and to another human being the exact nature of our wrongs.

6. Were entirely ready to have God remove all these defects of character.

7. Humbly asked Him to remove our shortcomings.

8. Made a list of all persons we had harmed, and became willing to make amends to them all.

9. Made direct amends to such people wherever possible, except when to do so would injure them or others.

10. Continued to take a daily inventory and when we were wrong, promptly admitted it.

11. Sought through prayer and meditation to improve our conscious contact with God as we understood Him, praying only for knowledge of His will for us and the power to carry that out.

12. Having had a spiritual awakening as the result of these steps, we tried to carry this message to others, and to practice these principles in all our affairs.

This Twelve Step process may appear overwhelming at first, but the longest journey begins with the first step. We found that working these steps one day at a time, sometimes even one minute at a time, leads to recovery. With the help of our Higher Power, The Twelve Steps of Phobics Anonymous, and the fellowship of our group, our lives began to change from isolation and fear to living calmly and serenely. We found that these steps require complete honesty, open mindedness and willingness. We experience the rewards of one phobic helping another as we consciously work toward recovery.

Serenity Prayer

"God, Grant me the serenity to

accept the things I cannot change,

courage to change the things I can

and wisdom to know the difference."

Remember

"Fear is the Opposite of Faith"

"Easy Does it"

"Keep it Simple"

"Let Go and Let God"

"One Day at a Time"

The Twelve Steps
Of Alcoholics Anonymous

1. We admitted we were powerless over alcohol that our lives had become unmanageable.

2. Came to believe that a Power greater than ourselves could restore us to sanity.

3. Made a decision to turn our will and our lives over to the care of God as we understood Him.

4. Made a searching and fearless moral inventory of ourselves.

5. Admitted to God, to ourselves, and to another human being the exact nature of our wrongs.

6. Were entirely ready to have God remove all these defects of character.

7. Humbly asked Him to remove our shortcomings.

8. Made a list of all persons we had harmed, and become willing to make amends to them all.

9. Made direct amends to such people wherever possible, except when to do so would injure them or others.

10. Continued to take personal inventory and when we were wrong promptly admitted it.

11. Sought through prayer and meditation to improve our conscious contact with God as we understood Him, praying only for knowledge of His will for us and the power to carry that out.

12. Having had a spiritual awakening as the result of these steps we tried to carry this message to alcoholics, and to practice these principles in all our affairs.

*REPRINTED WITH PERMISSION OF
ALCOHOLICS ANONYMOUS WORLD SERVICES, INC.*

2

Current Treatment Modalities

"The only thing we have to fear is fear itself - nameless, unreasoning, unjustified terror, which paralyzes needed efforts to convert retreat into advance."

- President Franklin D. Roosevelt
1933, First Inaugural Address to the Nation

Current Treatment Modalities

We in Phobics Anonymous view the individual as a whole person when he or she is functioning in balance in the following four areas: physically, emotionally (or another term, psychologically) mentally, (or we could say intellectually), and spiritually.

An appropriate analogy would be to look at a table with four legs. The table symbolizes the individual. One leg stands for physical well-being, one for emotional wellbeing, one for mental well-being, and one for spiritual wellbeing. If one of these legs is broken, the table will not stand. It will be unbalanced.

We look at ourselves this way in dealing with our phobias. We try to determine which area is weak or unbalanced and then use the appropriate treatment modality. More often than not, we phobics found that each area of our being needed to be addressed and treated.

Before we venture into our spiritual approach to recovery through applying *The Twelve Steps of Phobics Anonymous*, we will take only a brief look at some of the other current treatment modalities.

Behavior Therapy is a currently accepted treatment

approach. It includes a variety of techniques that help people modify their unwanted behavior.

Exposure Therapy is utilized as a procedure wherein the individual is gradually exposed to feared situations. It is a process of gradual desensitization. As clients confront feared situations, they employ relaxation techniques. Deep breathing, visualization, positive affirmations are only a few tools used in exposure. Patients learn skills for riding out a panic attack, such as counting objects or holding a trinket, any practice to help one get through the attack, shifting the focus away from its symptoms and becoming grounded into the now.

Cognitive Therapy emphasizes a phobics' way of thinking: We phobics got into the habit of catastrophic thinking - focusing on the negative, listening in, and misinterpreting our physical symptoms and therefore, anticipating the worst. We told ourselves, "I can't." We said, "What if?" in a million ways. What if I have to flee? What if I die? What if I embarrass myself? What if I lose control?

Cognitive restructuring takes time. It involves rewriting the script, thus changing the program in our mental computers with positive mental imagery and affirmations. Cognitive therapy helps to break the vicious cycle of the "What if ..." Syndrome.

The Self Care Approach of Dr. Claire Weekes' deserves mention for one self-treating. Reading her works increases the phobic's intellectual awareness of the condition. The four essential concepts advocated by Dr. Weekes are:

1. Face - Do not run away
2. Accept - Do not fight
3. Float - Do not tense
4. Let time pass - Do not be impatient.

Medication or Pharmacology is another currently accepted form of treatment <u>but always in conjunction with other therapies, and always taking into account the "Reward verses Risk" factor.</u> Several medications have been found to play positive roles in the treatment of anxiety disorders. The drugs prescribed to treat various anxiety disorders fall into these classes: benzodiazepines, antihistamines, tricyclic antidepressants, MAO inhibitors, and bet-andrenergic blockers. Medicines and dosage levels vary from individual to individual. It often takes time as well as trial and error to determine what actually works best for each phobic.

Recent research has shown panic disorder is a real, physical condition. Brain scans, which measure brain activity, have shown panic sufferers have higher than normal activity in the region of the brain which makes adrenaline, a hormone that helps the body respond to dangerous or stressful situations. This may create a lower threshold for a built-in alarm system, causing the alarm to go off even when there is no danger: The "Fight or Flight Syndrome". Because this evidence gives researchers a better idea of the brain chemicals involved in panic, they may be better able to choose new drugs which could block panic attacks.

Many phobics are pill-phobic and fear loss of control from using medication. Phobics often resist medicines or use minimal doses. We need education and support in this area. It could be safe to say: at this time, the accepted mode of treatment is exposure therapy in conjunction with pharmacology. We offer the Twelve Step as a vital adjunct approach with proven results.

Assertiveness Training which has its roots in the principle of Pavlovian conditioning, is another treatment utilized. Since phobics tend to be people pleasers and respond out of fear, we have trouble saying "No".

Flooding is a technique of Implosive Therapy - literally throwing oneself into the feared situation until there is no longer the phobic response. Suffering phobics are very fragile and sensitive people. Any flooding technique should be used with professional, empathetic care. Of course, there must be willingness on the part of the phobic to participate in this controversial technique.

Nutritional Therapy and **exercise** are advantageous. Most phobics find that much caffeine or sugar contributes to panic attacks. A well-balanced diet, proper vitamins and minerals are known to effect our behavior. It is also clearly evident physical exercise - walking, biking, etc. - help reduce anxiety levels and offset the often accompanying depression.

Psychotherapy and psychoanalysis based on the writing of Sigmund Freud's theories of personal relations and analytic theory are utilized in the field. It has been the experience of many suffering phobics that psychoanalysis alone is not sufficient. Most phobics feel that delving into their past can be too time-consuming and expensive. They are also more concerned in dealing with the present and immediate skills.

Self-help support groups are successful and beneficial. We find one suffering phobic helping another in a small group setting offers tremendous benefits. Participants in a self-help group hold a common trait - overwhelming panic. People grow and improve much more easily around people who have been through the same things. The fact of one phobic functioning well gives another phobic hope.

Anyone is welcome in a small self-help group, without intimidation or pressure. They attend when they want, which is very important. A major step toward recovery is the phobic's desire and willingness to reach out for help. Giving and receiving help in a warm, nurturing situation enhances recovery. By helping other phobics in a group, the suffering phobic shifts the focus away from himself and finds relief.

Another benefit of a group is that contact with other human beings is an antidote to loneliness. Through weekly meetings and telephone calls between members, the group provides a safety net, which is vital to someone in a crisis or panic state. Self-help groups are a unique complement to, rather than a replacement for, therapy, medical care, and other treatment modalities.

We have only briefly touched upon current approaches. There are many excellent readings in each field to further educate the suffering phobic. For our purposes here, we give credence to each modality and feel very happy and enthusiastic to present an adjunct program in *The Twelve Steps of Phobics Anonymous.*

3

The Twelve Steps

"Believe that life is worth living and your belief will help create the fact."

- William James

The Twelve STEPS
of Phobics Anonymous

1. We admitted that we were powerless over Fear - that our lives had become unmanageable.

2. Came to believe that a power greater than ourselves could restore us to wholeness.

3. Made a decision to turn our will and our lives over to the care of God, as we understood Him.

4. Made a searching and fearless moral inventory of ourselves.

5. Admitted to God, to ourselves, and to another human being the exact nature of our wrongs.

6. Were entirely ready to have Him remove all these defects of character.

7. Humbly asked Him to remove our shortcomings.

8. Made a list of all persons we had harmed, and became willing to make amends to them all.

9. Made direct amends to such people wherever possible, except when to do so would injure them or others.

10. Continued to take a daily inventory and when we were wrong, promptly admitted it.

11. Sought through prayer and meditation to improve our conscious contact with God as we understood Him, praying only for knowledge of His will for us and the power to carry that out.

12. Having had a spiritual awakening as the result of these steps, we tried to carry this message to others, and to practice these principles in all our affairs.

STEP 1

"We Admitted We Were Powerless Over Fear - That Our Lives Had Become Unmanageable."

We found that fear became personified, took itself on as an entity - our enemy. It seemed to control us in the most unlikely and unwanted places and situations. Its severe symptoms of panic and terror paralyzed us and made us feel totally out of control. It proved to be very embarrassing. What would someone think of this irrational fear in somewhat "normal" situations? We felt crazy, like we were going to die. We wanted to escape, to run away and hide, never having to experience that devastating feeling again. We carefully monitored all our bodily symptoms and the exact places and times these symptoms would likely appear. We tried to manage by avoiding any place or anybody we felt might trigger the dreaded response.

We sought out counselors, psychologists, and psychiatrists. We read everything we could get our hands on self-help books, magazine articles, research papers etc. Many of us kept our fears secret. Nobody seemed to understand our "crazy" fears and behaviors. Some of us took medications which seemed to help with symptoms and blocked the panic. Many of us switched from doctor to doctor, medicine to medicine, to find relief. The perimeter of our world became narrower and narrower. Sometimes, with the aid of pills and/or alcohol, we could cut the edge.

We came to a point when we tried to fight the fear - we tried to intellectualize it and finally admitted we, alone, were powerless over this enemy. Our lives were narrow and confined. Many of us became prisoners in our own homes, afraid to go out, afraid to answer the door or the phone. We became afraid to live and afraid to die. Our lives had indeed become unmanageable.

The motivating force in our lives had become fear. Some of us found that our own worst fears came true. Deep within each one of us was a terrible fear of abandonment, separation, rejection, and loss. We felt inadequate, totally incapable, and very unhappy. Sadness over this unexplainable fear led some of us to the depths of depression. Anti-life feelings pervaded the mind. Why live if you cannot be free to be normal? The most tragic situations ended in suicide or at least in the attempt. We needed something more powerful than this enemy, fear, to help us. By the time we finally admitted we were powerless, months, years, even decades, went by for some of us. We became painfully aware that our lives were unmanageable. The more we tried to fight it or intellectualize, as if in quicksand, the deeper we sank into our affliction.

STEP 2

"Came To Believe That A Power Greater
Than Ourselves Could Restore Us To Sanity."

It was at this point that we looked to a Higher Power to help us, something outside of ourselves. We needed help and realized we could not eliminate the fear by ourselves. How strange it is that we can readily accept the power of some unseen force like electricity yet not accept our Higher Power and the energy for healing and growth. Some of us prayed to a Higher Power of our individual understanding. We became open, receptive to help. We began to look up. We realized that lack of confidence in a Higher Power had caused us to struggle through life. If our lives were truly meant to be joyful and productive, then a Higher Power could help us. We had to walk by faith, not fear. We took little baby steps at this time. Our fear had become a habit a learned response. We were conditioned to our panic responses. Even the thought of our phobic situation could bring on the symptoms. But, in our misery, we came to hope, to believe we could once more function as before.

We really did not like to think our sanity was in jeopardy. Yet inside we knew something was wrong. Our phobic responses were neither normal nor rational. They debilitated us. Cut us off from much of life. New experiences, exciting travels, invitations, better jobs became a source of anticipatory anxiety. All areas of our lives were cut short. We knew that being restored to wellness would mean having once again the ability to participate fully in life as life was meant to be - a joy, not a chore! New doors and broader horizons would open up. Our inward eyeballs would turn outward. Free from fear, we could live a better way, a saner way, a more manageable way. Apprehension, anxiety, confusion, instability, and despair would no longer exist.

A power greater than ourselves is a broad term to many. Some people, extremely disillusioned, disappointed and feeling betrayed, would not accept the concept that a power greater than ourselves could decide the direction of our lives. Others could accept God as our Higher Power but had little idea of what this relationship meant. Still others found a Higher Power through the support group itself or through aspects of nature. This power, whether through the order of nature, the strength of the group, or through belief and faith in God, could restore us to sanity. Many members testified to their victory over fear as receiving a gift, a significant spiritual experience, or by noticing as they lived the Twelve Steps, one day at a time, that, by grace, their fears were diminishing. They were gradually being restored, renewed, and becoming stronger.

"Acceptance"

Is the answer to all my problems.

When I am disturbed, it is because

I find some person, place, thing,or

situation - some fact of my life

unacceptable to me. I can find no

serenity until I accept that person,

place, thing, or situation as being

exactly the way it is supposed to be

at this moment.

Nothing, absolutely nothing,

happens in God's world by mistake;

unless I accept life completely

on life's terms, I cannot be happy.

I need to concentrate not so much on

what needs to be changed in the

world as on what needs to be changed

in me and in my attitudes.

STEP 3

"Made A Decision To Turn Our Will And Our Lives Over To The Care Of God, As We Understood Him."

With the first step, we admitted our problem. With the second step, we came to believe. The third step is a key step. It opens the door to recovery. This step involves a choice, a decision. It involves surrender. We spend most of our scattered lives conjugating three verbs - to want, to have, and to do. Forgetting none of these verbs have any ultimate significance except so far as they are transcended by, and included in the fundamental verb, "to be". Being, not wanting, having, and doing is the essence of a spiritual life.

As most human beings, we phobics were very masterful at controlling people and our surroundings. Actually, our trying to control according to our way or our wills ultimately led to many of our anxieties and frustrations. Things didn't always turn out as we planned. Our attempts at avoidance, control, and self-will did not free us from our irrational fears. Some of us kept our circles so narrow we deluded ourselves into feeling okay. But the okay feeling was a poor excuse, a limited version of living. Our phobias and fears were so unpleasant we often did not face them. We were victims of self-delusion. The self-delusion told us we were okay and things were not that bad. But as the phobias and panic symptoms progressively got worse, our world progressively narrowed and some of us became desperate. It takes a great deal of courage to reach out for help. It seemed easier just to stay inside the safety zone we had erected. Yet for others, taking that little step outside the safety zone or the comfort area meant the beginning of a whole new life.

Surrendering in the third step is turning our will and our lives over to the care of a Higher Power. Stop trying to do it alone. Many of our conflicts come from trying to deal with the spiritual and practical aspects of our lives as two separate entities instead of accepting them as parts of a whole. It is the principle element in hooking up to a positive, powerful source. It is letting go of our fears; of turning them over; of releasing them. It is taking ourselves, the plug, and putting it into the power circuit. Carrying this heavy burden on our own shoulders weighed us down, finally bringing us to our knees. What a relief to give the burden away to our Higher Power.

Of course, we also had to give away our self-will and compulsion for control. This is hard to do when we have been so used to doing things "my way". We usually found when we meddled again or took back our burdens, manipulating, trying to control, we got fearful again. So we practiced letting go of our fears every day. We surrendered anew each morning. We put our lives and wills in care of our Higher Power and learned to accept, to trust, and to let go.

Third Step Prayer

"God, I offer myself to thee - to build with me and to do with me as thou wilt. Relieve me of the bondage of self, that I may better do thy will. Take away my difficulties, that victory over them may bear witness to those I would help of Thy Power, Thy Love, and Thy Way of life. May I do Thy will always!"

STEP 4

"Made A Searching And Fearless Moral Inventory Of Ourselves".

This step involves taking a hard look in the mirror. It had been so easy in the past to take the focus off ourselves and put it onto other people or situations. By focusing on everything but our own selves, we managed to avoid seeing our own shortcomings. We could easily rationalize and find other things to blame for our difficulties. We could find reasons for our phobic responses from past traumas or hurts. Yet we found by just blaming others, we did not manage to get well. We just remained stuck in our own illness.

Taking the fourth step was a step toward personal responsibility. It is a step in growing up;in uncovering self-deception; in raising our self-esteem by recognizing our assets, talents, and abilities. It involves facing reality and knowing who we really are.

This inventory involves both the good part of ourselves; our assets, as well as the negative part, or those liabilities which keep us stuck. We begin to see certain patterns in our lives. We see where certain motivating forces have caused us to repeat self-destructive behaviors over and over again. We phobics found many of our actions were motivated by fear. Who we spent time with, where we went, what we did were, to a large extent, predicted by our level of fear. In our personal inventories we had to face our self-defeating behaviors. We found our inventory took a concerted effort at honesty. We found it was painful to get honest - brutally honest - with ourselves. As we began to see more clearly our defects, we felt sad, remorseful, and sorry for things we had done wrong. We were able to acknowledge real guilt and to also see where we assumed a lot of false guilt.

We found we often denied our own needs and assets in trying to please others. We were master people pleasers and co-dependents. We really feared if we did not please enough, we would be rejected or abandoned. This terrified us. All the panic symptoms emerged at the thought of being alone, forsaken. We realized we did not really know how good we are, how valuable we are. We lacked confidence, self-esteem, and proper self-images. We needed to see, and understand our worth.

Our inventory showed highly sensitive, perfectionistic, caring, creative, people - pleasing, imaginative people with poor self-esteem, lack of confidence, motivated by worry, fear and guilt. We began to see clearly how these characteristics had affected our life choices. We made an inventory of misdeeds - areas we knew where we had compromised our standards. Surprisingly enough, we found where we had compromised our standards, values, morals, and honesty, we had experienced more phobic symptoms or panic attacks. It seemed as if the easily rationalized misdeeds we had performed had adversely affected our mental health. We knew we needed to "clean house". We made a commitment to "clean up our act," one day at a time, and in so doing, to accept ourselves for the worthwhile, valuable human beings we are.

"The Difference"

I got up early one morning and rushed right into the day.
I had so much to accomplish that I didn't have time to pray.
Problems just tumbled around and heavier came each task.
"Why doesn't God help me?" I wondered. He said, "But you didn't ask."
I wanted to see joy and beauty, but the day tolled on, gray and bleak.
I wondered why God didn't show me. He said, "But you didn't seek."
I tried to come into God's presence. I used all my keys at the lock.
God gently and lovingly chided, "My child, you didn't knock."
I woke up early this morning and paused before entering the day.
I had so much to accomplish that I had to take time to pray.

STEP 5

"Admitted To God, To Ourselves, And To Another Human Being The Exact Nature Of Our Wrongs."

This step could be called the confession step or getting it off one's chest. All through history, people have found a cleansing effect in admitting wrongs. It is like taking the inner guilt and giving it away. It is taking the heavy burden off one's own shoulders. It leaves one feeling free, light, and able to take a deep breath. It is a good feeling to get clean.

We found those deceptions buried deep were part of our unhappiness. It is only by seeing the wrongs and admitting them that we are led to being set free of their erosion. We found where we were once blind, we began to see.

It takes courage to admit our wrongs. It is easier to admit them to a Higher Power and ask forgiveness, but we found to admit to another trusted person took looking straight in the eyes. It meant taking off our mask, feeling the pain, swallowing one's pride, admitting we are not perfect, we don't know everything, and we have made mistakes.

It was important to choose a trustworthy person with whom we could establish a confident reliance. What we found after disclosing our wrongs was the other person admired us, felt more comfortable with us, accepted us.

By admitting our wrongs, we said "Hey, I'm just human, I've made mistakes. I'm not better nor worse than you". We turned into transmitters instead of receivers. We opened the door to communicating on a genuine level. Once we gained insight into ourselves, we found we could relate on a more intimate level. We became more transparent, more vulnerable. We gradually stopped the game playing. We stopped pretending we felt okay and we stopped avoiding telling the truth.

Once we admitted our irrational fear, we took a great deal of power away from that fear. It was a relief to "come out of the closet". What a relief not to keep those devastating feelings and symptoms a secret. We found we could then begin to become victorious over our fear. We could talk to someone. We were not alone! We had our Higher Power and we had each other. No longer were we totally isolated in our self-made prisons.

"Just for Today"

Just for today I will try to live through this day only, and not tackle all my problems at once. I can do something for twelve hours that would appall me if I felt that I had to keep it up for a lifetime.

Just for today I will be happy. This assumes to be true what Abraham Lincoln said, that "Most folks are as happy as they make up their minds to be."

Just for today I will adjust myself to what is, and not try to adjust everything to my own desires. I will take my "luck" as it comes, and fit myself to it.

Just for today I will try to strengthen my mind. I will study. I will learn something useful. I will not be a mental loafer. I will read something that requires effort, thought and concentration.

Just for today I will exercise my soul in three ways: I will do somebody a good turn, and not get found out; if anybody knows of it, it will not count. I will do at least two things I don't want to do - just for exercise. I will not show anyone that my feelings are hurt; they may be hurt, but today I will not show it.

Just for today I will be agreeable. I will look as well as I can, dress becomingly, keep my voice low, be courteous, criticize not one bit. I won't find fault with anything, nor try to improve or regulate anybody but myself.

Just for today I will have a program. I may not follow it exactly, but I will have it. I will save myself from two pests: hurry and indecision.

Just for today I will have a quiet half hour all by myself, and relax. During this half hour, sometime, I will try to get a better perspective of my life.

Just for today I will be unafraid. Especially I will not be afraid to enjoy what is beautiful, and to believe that as I give to the world, so the world will give to me.

STEP 6

"Were Entirely Ready To Have God Remove All These Defects Of Character."

What does it mean to become, "entirely ready to have a Higher Power remove our defects of character"? This question brings to mind what does the word entirely ready mean? Okay, I have admitted my wrongs to my Higher Power, to myself, and to another human being. But what must I do to become entirely ready?

We phobics found that we could not become entirely ready on our own accord. We need our Higher Power and other people. Through a daily surrender to our Higher Power, through willingness, and through a searching heart, we place ourselves in a position for change. We must become clay.

We give up self-will trying to do things our way by our self-will. We seek a Higher Power, a greater wisdom, and strength to guide us. We acknowledge our inept attempts at controlling our lives and the lives of others, our futile attempts at controlling our fears, phobias and panic symptoms. We offer up our fears, the desires of our heart. We seek peace. We become more and more humble.

Becoming entirely ready takes time, a different amount of time for each person. We have been so accustomed to our way, our will, our masks, our walls, our facades, our defenses, they do not all come down overnight. Yet gradually, as we open our minds and hearts to our Higher Power, we begin to see the nature of our wrongs. We are gradually revealed to ourselves. Our motives, our choices, our wrong doings, become apparent. This is truly a humbling experience.

We phobics realize we are motivated by fear. Our life choices are predicated on fear. We let fear be our guide. As we realize we are living half-truths, prisoners and captives of fear, we become ready to have this terrible defect of character removed. Fear is a lie. Fear is deceit. Fear robs us. We realized our lives of fear were living a lie. We became ready to refuse to live this lie. Yet we knew we could not remove this character defect alone.

Sufficiently humbled, we appealed to our Higher Power with belief and thankfulness and asked Him to remove this defect of fear.

STEP 7

"Humbly Asked Him To Have
Our Shortcomings Removed."

We have taken our inventory, admitted our wrongs, and become ready for our Higher Power to remove our defects of character. With these preparatory steps, we have been brought to a place of humility. We are at a vantage point of looking up to our Higher Power.

As phobics, we tried every conceivable way to control our behaviors. We hid them. We studied them. We tried to intellectualize them. We psychoanalyzed them. We avoided all threatening situations and contacts. We gutted it out. We cried. We fought. We hid. We felt like we were dying, going crazy, or going to lose control until finally, at the point of surrender, we gave up. We began to let our Higher Power do the job. We opened ourselves to a strength greater than our own.

In this abject humility, we came to our Higher Power. We asked our Higher Power to remove our shortcomings. We would probably easily agree that Fear was one of our greatest shortcomings. Irrational fear had thwarted, twisted and tried to destroy our lives. Along with fear came other accompanying shortcomings that kept us from experiencing a full life.

We experienced unyielding depression because our seemingly hopeless phobias kept us down - dejected, sad, isolated, despairing, suicidal. Depression often led to other complications like using alcohol or drugs to self-medicate. Many phobics developed another problem - addiction. It is common knowledge addiction leads to all types of character compromises and unacceptable behavior.

To unravel these series of shortcomings all based on one lie - Fear - took a power greater than ourselves. Looking at this mess, we humbly asked our Higher Power to remove our shortcomings.

Seventh Step Prayer

My Creator, I am now willing that

you should have all

of me, good and bad. I pray that

you now remove from me

every single defect of character

which stands in the way of

my usefulness to you and my

fellows. Grant me strength, as

I go out from here to do your

bidding. Amen.

STEP 8

"Made A List Of All Persons We Had Harmed, And Became Willing To Make Amends To Them All."

Step 8 is an action step. It is admirable to recognize and admit our defects of character and surely our Higher Power is instrumental in removing them, but we have some work to do here. As we have been "cleaning house", uncluttering the past agenda of our lives, and rewriting our scripts, we found injured parties strewn around.

In the process of becoming free or a new person not weighted down with fear and guilt, we realized we had apologies, restitutions and reconciliations to make.

A simple way to begin this step is to do exactly as it says. Get a sheet of paper and a pen and sit down. Think through your life. Try to be as honest with yourself as possible. Remember, we are all victims of self-deception. Let's try to put rationalizing aside.

Examine relationships with other people; family, friends, co-workers. Look for any less than true motives in dealing with people. Some misconducts will be glaringly evident. Gross deceits or immoral behaviors, or violent actions will all be too readily recognized. Being convicted of our unethical behavior is very painful. We suffer shame and remorse at how many people we have hurt by our behavior, either intentionally or unintentionally. Yet, it is essential for the sake of serenity, peace of mind and restitution to go through this process.

When our list is made, we need to find appropriate times and ways to make amends. If an outright reminder of the offense or if an apology would create more hurt for the offended person and his family, it is better left unsaid. Acknowledge the offense to your Higher Power and be aware of that pitfall in the future.

Many amends can be made with a brief note, a phone call or a visit. Sometimes monetary retribution needs to be made or some other good turn. An injured party is given a great gift when an offender makes amends. The injured party feels less resentful, less self-pity, less unhappiness. It is a privilege to bring joy to another person by making amends. How lucky we are to be able to make this world a happier place by bringing reconciliation and peace into our lives.

STEP 9

"Made Direct Amends To Such People Wherever Possible, Except When To Do So Would Injure Them Or Others."

Now our list is made up of people we have harmed. We begin the process of making amends. There is no set pattern or amount of time required. It will be different for each person.

As we phobics realize the people we have hurt or harmed by being motivated and dominated by fear, we will experience a real sorrow. We will be deeply saddened by our actions. We will experience a heartfelt brokenness. Because of this, we will be able to honestly say we are sorry to those we have hurt. We will not add more hurt by revealing the misdeeds; if the revelation would add more hurt, then we should not be inclined to give the information.

Financial amends are rather clear cut. Forms of restitution can be made, but how do you make amends for a betrayal, for abandoning someone, for taking a life, for some misdeed which deprived someone of their happiness? When the desire is in the heart, we found making amends could take a variety of forms. Often an amend took the form of warning someone who was heading on the wrong course. We shared our own experience and thereby helped others to see what consequences their actions could incur.

Making amends can take place by working on community projects or social causes. We can make life a little easier for someone else. Take the drunk driver who kills a child. He later makes amends by working in the field of public awareness against drunk driving. The child is dead, but the offender can work toward better future conditions.

Sometimes we just can't think of an amend we can make. It is then we offer it up to our Higher Power, whose power and grace can bring restitution and reconciliation where we cannot.

Because fear is such a learned behavior pattern, we phobics found we had to confront it almost on a daily basis. In our daily inventory, we had to admit where fear motivated our choices. We had to aggressively recognize it and see it for what it was, fear, and for what it is - a lie! We had to call a spade a spade. We had to refuse to be dominated by fear - to be dominated by a lie. As we accepted it on a daily basis our fears grew less and less.

Two Days We Should Not Worry About

Yesterday: with its mistakes and heartaches. They are gone forever.

Tomorrow: Is the other day. It has problems and possibilities, but until the sun rises, it is unborn and unreal.

Today is the only day that matters. Only when we bear the burdens of those other two days are we likely to fail.

STEP 10

"Continued To Take A Daily Inventory And When We Were Wrong, Promptly Admitted It."

We phobics were always looking for a quick cure, the thing which would make us better immediately. Medication was a pretty good tool for this. We went to doctors - many, many doctors - with our symptoms. We were given a myriad of prescriptions. We had many different medicines i.e. heart, sugar level, anti-depressants, anti-psychotic, and tranquilizers. We found for many of us the tranquilizers were effective in blocking panic symptoms.

Some phobics stopped their recovery process with tranquilizers. Relieved of the most debilitating symptoms, these phobics felt free and wonderful in pursuing the things they once feared. But somewhere in their mind was the question: What if I can't get my medication? What if the doctor doesn't prescribe my tranquilizer? As long as medical theory authorized the use of certain medicines, we found a wonderful panacea.

Again, there were phobics who were pill phobic and fearful of going to a doctor. These people would never consider taking any prescribed medication since they could not even take aspirin.

Some phobics found themselves chemically dependent on their medications. Addictive phobics abused their pills and found themselves in a real mess - a phobic addicted to tranquilizers. Often hand in hand with tranquilizers came the self-medication with alcohol. A pill and cocktail and no more anxiety. How very captivating this cure. But it led to its own destructive ends.

We phobics needed a cure which was lasting and far-reaching, not a bandaid approach. Medicine which masked the symptoms for the immediate time, was necessary, and effective for some phobics. Alcohol was a temporary anxiety reliever. But what could alleviate our anxiety once and for all? What could give us a lifestyle of peace, serenity, and confidence? Who could set us free from the bondage of fear? We found the answer in the Twelve Steps and our Higher Power.

Some of us approached working the Twelve Steps as you would take a course in school. You read them, study them, memorize them, and it's all over. Untrue!! This is not the case.

The Twelve Steps of Phobics Anonymous is a lifelong spiritual program for living. The steps are something which becomes integrated into our minds, hearts, and actions. Each of us is an unfinished product on which our Higher Power is continually at work.

We must practice the Twelve Steps over and over. We go in and out of the steps as needed. We bathe ourselves with the Twelve Steps spiritually. We allow our Higher Power and the Twelve Step to permeate our lives. We begin to live the steps. Gradually, we are transformed, renewed, revitalized, and set free.

As Step 10 states, we take a daily inventory of ourselves. A good time to do this is in the evening before we go to sleep. We go through the day and see if we've hurt anyone, or if were dishonest. We ask our Higher Power to show us where we might have been in error. We don't try to make excuses. We admit where we were wrong. We plan to make amends quickly. We found we did not want to do wrong. We wanted to keep short accounts with our Higher Power. When we did, through our humanness, we wanted to quickly get it out of the way. We examined our hearts and minds for any wrongdoing each day and through the grace of our Higher Power we found gradually we could find less and less wrongdoings. With thankfulness to our Higher Power and each other, we were experiencing a new life.

STEP 11

"Sought Through Prayer And Meditation To Improve Our Conscious Contact With God As We Understood Him, Praying Only For Knowledge Of His Will For Us And The Power To Carry That Out."

This step becomes a part of our daily living. Having realized that we were unable to solve our problems alone and having surrendered ourselves to our Higher Power, we found that we needed to take daily time in communion with our Higher Power. This requires personal effort and personal choice. We had to be willing to be filled, to be guided, to be nourished, to become spiritually hungry. We found we needed to nourish this hunger on a daily basis. This meant taking the time to be with our Higher Power. We found if we sought our Higher Power, we found Him. Prayer and meditation were the tools to expel from our lives the thoughts and acts which kept us in bondage.

Because so many of our choices and experiences had been determined by our fear, we had really created chaos. Often in our prayer time, we really did not see a way out, a solution. We often did not know what we really wanted. We became more aware of how very little we did know. Our minds were too troubled, clouded, and fearful, to receive the signals given until we gradually ceased to ask for specific things and began to ask for knowledge of our Higher Power's will for us.

All things will work for the best outcome. All the pieces of our lives will form a perfectly fitted puzzle. We found our Higher Power will give us dramatic transformation, renewal, redemption, and reconciliation. We could never accomplish this on our own accord. We found our Higher Power was doing for us what we could not do ourselves.

Our Fears grew less and less. As we learned the will of our Higher Power, we prayed for the strength to carry it out. We phobics knew that to have the ability to carry out our Higher Power's will meant we had to be bold. We had to act in faith, not fear, to be able to take risks. We asked our Higher Power for this courage.

Prayer is an active, not passive, experience. It involves looking upward, reaching out and putting forth the desires of our heart. It involves petitioning forgiveness. It is an appeal for help. Our prayer was approached humbly but with heartfelt anguish and surrender.

In our prayers, we had to believe. Without belief in our Higher Power, we could not stand in faith for an answer to our prayers. We had to believe in our Higher Power's love for us, in the desire to see us joyful, in the gift of an abundant life. We had to know we are worthy, we are valuable, we are forgiven, and we are loved! We had to be absolved from guilt. We had to know our rightful place, our inheritance.

We had to know who we are.

Meditation is the listening part of our contact with our Higher Power. We often became so busy we never stopped to listen. We did not become still and wait for knowledge of our Higher Power's will. In meditating, we stopped. We spent time with our Higher Power - quiet time. We became still. We waited. We heard the still, small voice. We began to see. We intuitively knew what we sought. We were amazed to understand the nearness of our Higher Power, the close presence at all times, not something distant and far away, but a power right here within us - never changing, never ending - always the same, always loving. A source just waiting to be tapped into by us.

STEP 12

"Having Had A Spiritual Awakening As The Result Of These Steps, We Tried To Carry This Message To Others, And To Practice These Principles In All Our Affairs."

The word "awakening" in this step infers we had been spiritually asleep. For we phobics, that meant many things but predominantly we could not see what was truth. We lived in doubt, fear, and despair. We lived in isolation. We could not discuss the reality of our natures. We were bound in our own prisons. We were living a lie.

Practicing these Twelve Steps, we began to see our real selves. A step at a time, we became more confident. Our Higher Power was helping us to see.

We saw our fear was a lie, a distortion, a deception, we had bought into. We had been rendered immobile and paralyzed. With our spiritual awakening, we became free. We were no longer afraid of people. We were no longer afraid of economic insecurity. We were not afraid of places or situations. We were given life and all its opportunities. Everything looked more beautiful, more exciting. We became optimistic, confident. Gradually, we embraced life rather than feared it.

There is no specific time for a spiritual awakening to occur. With some, it is a long process. For others, it happens fairly quickly, but we knew when we experienced this awakening.

We did the footwork of practicing the steps. Our Higher Power gave us the gift - our freedom from fears. We found we could help our recovery by giving away what we had learned. Therefore, we helped other suffering phobics. Now living outside of our isolation, we established closer personal fellowship with others. We became more service oriented. We realized we are each of us angels with only one wing and we can fly only by embracing each other.

We also found we had to practice the principles of the Twelve Steps in all our affairs. We could not compromise. To compromise would mean relapse, setbacks and backtracking. We liked our new freedom, wanted to share with others, and experience new joy.

The focus on self shifted to a focus on our Higher Power and on others. We did not wallow around in self-analysis. We lost interest in conflict, in worry. We lived more simply, more truthfully. When faced with doubt, fear, or anxiety, we recognized it for what it is, a deception. We refused to accommodate it. When we believed we were genuinely free of our fears, their power over us slipped away. The tools of these

Twelve Steps, the help of our Higher Power and the support of other phobics led us down the path toward recovery.

We realized a new spontaneity in our actions. We lost interest in judging ourselves and others. We lived in the moment, enjoying life. We appreciated our blessings. We felt a new connection with people and nature. We reached out in love. We smiled through the eyes of the heart.

4

Affirmations for the Anxiety Addict

"The greatest revolution

of our generation

is the discovery that

human beings,

by changing the inner

attitudes of their minds,

can change the outer

aspects of their lives."

- William James
19th Century Psychologist
and Philosopher

AFFIRMATIONS FOR THE ANXIETY ADDICT
Also Relaxation, Diaphragmatic Breathing,
Creative Visualization, and Meditation

Our minds have a vast reservoir of potential, unbelievable power and yet research shows that only 10% is used at any given time. Affirmations are an effective technique to tap into a part of this awesome power and put it to work. They are mental tools which can be used to overcome physical symptoms enabling us to deal more positively with fear, anxiety, panic and phobic situations. We have tried and failed to heal ourselves by manipulating our environment. True healing must begin on the inside.

For those not familiar with what affirmations are, they are strong positive thoughts or statements we deliberately program into our subconscious mind to replace the old, negative thinking which has plagued us for so long. Negative thoughts are like weeds which choke the seeds and halt the growth of the recovery process. What the mind can conceive, if you really believe, you can achieve. WE ARE WHAT WE THINK!

Change happens quickly when positive affirmations are used because a thought is a very mobile and quick form of light energy. They are manifested instantly, thus allowing us to rewrite our scripts, change our tapes, and reprogram our computers. Subsequently we replace negative, stale, outdated, fearful thoughts with more positive ideas and concepts.

We are the writers, directors, producers, and stars of our life scripts. We are not puppets, but active participants. Affirmations are a way of unconsciously rehearsing a thought which eventually will become more accessible to our conscious mind. Then we can act on it to produce the results we desire.

Before I go any further and suggest some examples of affirmations for the phobic, let me present the most effective methods of using them.

1. Always affirm in a positive way to create the most positive image. <u>NEVER</u> reinforce the negative. *Example:* I am now able to drive on the freeway. <u>NOT</u>, I am no longer fearful of driving {negative}.

2. Affirmations are always phrased in the present. *Example:* I am now able to go to the market. <u>NOT</u>, I will be able to go to the market.

3. Affirmations, to be most effective, should be short and simple. *Examples:* I am a whole, healthy human being. I am capable of changing. I accept all of my feelings. I deserve love, peace, prosperity, and serenity.

4. Always choose an affirmation which makes you comfortable. *Example:* I am not alone. I am one with my Higher Power.

5. Affirmations affirm what you want (positive), not what you want to get rid of (negative). *Example:* I am able to face today fearlessly. <u>NOT</u>, I want to lose the ability to worry.

6. Affirmations will get you your desired results, but only if you believe in them and put your full mental and emotional energy into them.

7. Affirmations should be done in a first, second, and third person format. (*Example:* I, <u>name</u>, am able to go to the party. You, <u>name</u>, are able to go to the party. He or she, <u>name</u>, is able to go to the party).

Don't expect instant results. Affirmations take time to work. They cannot be rushed. It may take days or weeks because you must choose with the conscious part of your mind to take control of the unconscious and this is accomplished by repeating the affirmations on a daily basis. The desired results are produced by repetition of the positive thoughts which lead to the reprogramming of your subconscious.

There are many different ways to practice affirmations. Here are some our group found most effective.

1. Write them down on 3 x 5 cards and carry them with you or tape them to the bathroom mirror or refrigerator door. Repeat them over and over again (but not by rote) on a daily basis. They can be spoken aloud or read silently to yourself.

2. Take a piece of paper and write them as you say them at least 15 times a day.

3. Tape your affirmations and play them back to yourself. Just listen to the tape or repeat your affirmations out loud as you listen to them.

4. Make up simple chants or songs expressing your affirmations and sing them sincerely and meaningfully. Try one or two affirmations a day at first. Don't overload yourself and really think about the meaning as you say or write them. Don't let it become a mechanical process.

One last note, affirmations which include a spiritual dimension are often more powerful, inspiring, and effective. (*Example:* My Higher Power is protecting me now. I have nothing to fear).

"Techniques for Thinking"

1. Keep it simple.
2. Practice cheerfulness.
3. Learn to like people.
4. Live and let live.
5. Don't take yourself so seriously.
6. Have a sense of humor.
7. Practice objectivity.
8. Forgive yourself.

Here is some "Food for Thought" used in our group that you might find helpful.

1. Wherever you are at this moment is exactly where you are supposed to be no matter how things may seem to appear.

2. Go with the flow.

3. Don't sweat the small stuff, & it's all small stuff.

4. Easy does it.

5. First things first.

6. Administer daily: self-love, self-care, self-acceptance.

7. Face your fear and the fear will disappear.

8. Even though at times it appears that life doesn't seem to be working, it is still working perfectly. There is no prescribed way for everyone. There is just your way for now until you choose another.

9. Our healing begins when we are willing to acknowledge and admit our problems.

10. Be like a postage stamp - stick to one thing until it gets to its destination.

Relaxation

It's a physical impossibility to be relaxed and anxious at the same time. Therefore, relaxation plays a vital role in our recovery process from fear and anxiety.

The definition of relaxation is to make or become less firm, tense, or strict. In this state, it is much easier to get in touch with your body and feelings. Daily functions such as thinking, heart rate, and excessive movement are slowed as a wave of calmness flows in and out with each breath.

There are numerous tapes and books containing relaxation exercises, so we will not describe any techniques or exercises here. The important thing to remember is when you practice relaxation, make sure you have a pleasant scene in mind and a place where you are safe, comfortable, and anxiety-free.

Some members of our group find it very difficult to relax. The letting go, loss of control, and relaxed feeling is so foreign to them it causes anxiety, but this can be overcome in time with practice.

Diaphragmatic Breathing

We can live without food, clothing and shelter, the basic necessities of life, for a short period of time, but we cannot live without breathing. It's something our bodies do without our help, but even though the first thing a child does when he is born is breathe, and we continue the process day and night, many of us breathe incorrectly, taking shallow breaths instead of long, deep ones. In times of stress and acute anxiety, we unconsciously hold our breaths or breathe very irregularly, causing hyperventilation, which in turn increases our panic symptoms.

The level of carbon dioxide in our blood plays a vital role in regulating our breathing. It is exhaled along with water vapor and oxygen is inhaled. The need to release carbon dioxide is actually what stimulates our breathing response.

Deep breathing, otherwise known as diaphragmatic breathing, completely fills our lungs with oxygen and enables us to relax more fully. To practice diaphragmatic breathing, take a long, slow, deep breath in through the nose to the count of four. Hold it for the count of four and then exhale slowly and completely to the count of four. As you exhale, you can feel the tension leave your body and a feeling of calmness result.

You can practice diaphragmatic breathing any time and any place you feel anxious. It requires no equipment. However, to obtain the most beneficial results, take time at home or at work, and place your body in a comfortable position. I suggest a chair with an upright back support. Keep your feet on the floor, hands and arms spread apart and palms open and facing upward.

Try this for a minimum of five minutes and see how the tension, fear, and anxiety flows out of your body each time you exhale. Then immerse yourself in the feeling of tranquility and calmness entering each time you inhale. In this relaxed state, your meditation exercises and affirmations will be better received by your subconscious mind and, thus, will be more effective.

Creative Visualization

Creative visualization is another very useful, constructive, and powerful tool which utilizes your imagination to create an idea, a mental picture, or a clear image of something you want in your life. It is the conscious, controlled directing of your imagination to produce whatever results you desire.

When we are anxious and fearful, we tend to attract the very feelings, experiences, and situations we are trying to avoid. What you resist persists. Conversely, when you direct your thoughts and your imagination in a positive way, positive results are then produced.

The word "visualization" means to make or become visible, to see or form a mental image. Some people don't actually "see" or form a mental image when they visualize. They "think" and this works just as well.

There are five basic steps which make creative visualization more effective:

1. Goal Setting - Choose a goal that you really believe in and can achieve in the near future. *Example:* Visualize yourself in the least terrifying phobic situation. Do this by listing a hierarchy of your fears and start with the least fearful experience. If you are afraid of spiders, start with visualizing yourself just looking at a picture of a spider and progress from there until you finally can see yourself holding a spider.

2. Picture very specifically and clearly your goal.

3. Focus on your objective or goal often whenever you happen to have some unstressful, quiet time.

4. Think about your goal in a positive, encouraging way, using affirmations which will allow you to make firm that which you are imagining.

5. Try to close your eyes and relax your body completely, either sitting or lying down in a comfortable position with no distractions.

Creative visualization is nothing more than a dress rehearsal of an event which takes place in your mind.

Meditation

Meditation is a powerful technique which has been used for thousands of years to halt or slow down the continual flow of negative, fearful thoughts constantly continuing inside our minds.

It is a process whereby one consciously and intentionally quiets the mind. This causes the emotions and the intellect to respond to the quiet consciousness which leads us back to our inner self. Our conscious mind must be still before our subconscious can be impressed by it.

Meditation enables us to learn relaxation and control our reactions and emotions in quiet moments so we can then be prepared to do the same in times of panic or other emergencies.

A new relationship is established by meditation. Energy becomes available from within. In this way, we can learn to rule our own bodies and escape from our bondage of fear. We learn to command both feeling and thought.

The tranquility gained through meditation carries into our daily lives. We can make decisions in calmness for the right reasons rather than hastily in a panic.

> *"Live your life, every day of it, with*
> *great expectations and great things will*
> *happen in your life daily."*

Here are seven hints to help you meditate:

1) Meditate by just being aware of yourself.
2) Monitor your thoughts.
3) Be very aware of your feelings.
4) Observe yourself.
5) Be patient and calm.
6) Quiet your fearful, racing thoughts.
7) Desire only to be able to live differently.

One of my students at Turnoff (The Residential Drug and Alcohol Recovery Center where I presently teach) wrote the following; I was so impressed with it, I am including it here with his permission.

"Meditation: Mind and Body Unite"

Siddhara Buddha once said to meditate is but to open spiritual channels in thy inner self. Meditation has been used as a way to relax and create an inner sanctuary for centuries. In this writer's opinion, meditation is a time for self. A relaxing time to be peaceful inside whether with my God or with myself.

Meditation has always been thought of as cultish or fanatical. I, too, shared this belief in the past. Part of this was the result of misinformation combined with unrealistic expectations. I personally have not yet been completely entranced visually nor had a dramatic spiritual encounter as is commonly believed. Yet I have found a peacefulness I never could reach with drugs or falsified religions. The art of meditation is individual and unique to each person. For me, it is the unity of spirit, mind, and body coming together in harmony with its surroundings. I wouldn't suggest it to anyone who has over-expectations for anything but an experience with someone precious and special: yourself.

-Jeff

5

Be Kind To Your Mind

Get Rid of "Stinking Thinking".

"The Mask"

Don't be fooled by me. Don't be fooled by the face I wear.

For I wear a mask, I wear a thousand masks, masks that I'm afraid to take off, and none of them is me.

Pretending is an art that's second nature to me, but don't be fooled, for God's sake, don't be fooled.

I give you the impression that I am secure, that all is sunny and unruffled with me, within as well as without, that confidence is my name and coolness my game, that the water's calm and I'm in command, and that I need no one. But don't believe me. Please.

My surface may be smooth, but my surface is my mask, my varying and ever-concealing mask.

Beneath lies no snugness, no complacence.

Beneath it dwells the real me, in confusion and fear, in aloneness, but I hide this, I don't want anybody to know it.

That's why I frantically create a mask to hide behind, a nonchalant, sophisticated facade, to help me pretend, to shield

The 12 Steps

me from the glance that knows. But such a glance is precisely my salvation, my only salvation. And I know it, that is if it's followed by acceptance, if it is followed by love.

It is the only thing that can liberate me, from myself, from my own self-built prison walls, from the barriers I so painstakingly erect.

It is the only thing that will assure me of what I can't assure myself, that I'm really worth something.

But I don't tell you this, don't dare, I'm afraid to.

I'm afraid that your glance will not be followed by love. I'm afraid that you'll think less of me, that you'll laugh. And your laugh would kill me.

I'm afraid that deep down I'm nothing, that I'm just no good, and that you will see this and reject me.

So I play my game, with a facade of assurance without, and trembling child within.

And so begins the parade of masks, the glittering but empty masks. And my life becomes a front.
I idly chatter to you in the suave tones of surface talk.

I tell you everything that's really nothing, and nothing of what's everything, of what's crying within me.

So, when I'm going through my routine, please don't be fooled by what I'm saying. Please listen carefully, and try to hear what I'm not saying, and what I'd like to be able to say, what for survival I need to say, but what I can't say.

Honestly, I dislike the superficial game I'm playing, the superficial phony game; I'd really like to be genuine and spontaneous and me - but you've got to help me. You've got to hold out your hand, even when that's the last thing I seem to want or need.

Only you can wipe away from my eyes that blank stare of the breathing dead.

Only you can call me into aliveness.

Each time you're kind, and gentle, and encouraging, each time you try to understand because you really care, my heart begins to grow wings, very small wings, very feeble wings, but wings.

With your sensitivity and sympathy, and your power of understanding, you can breathe life into me, I want you to know that.

I want you to know how important you are to me, how you can be a creator of the person that's in me if you choose to.

Please choose to.

You alone can break down the wall behind which I tremble, you alone can remove my mask, you alone can release me from my lonely prison.

So do not pass me by. Please don't pass me by. It will not be easy for you.

A long conviction of worthlessness builds strong walls.

The nearer you approach me, the blinder I may strike back. It's irrational, but despite what the book says about man, I'm irrational. I fight against the very thing I cry out for. But I am told that love is stronger than strong walls.

In this lies my hope, my only hope.

Please try to beat down these walls with firm hands, but with gentle hands, for a child is very sensitive.

Who am I, you may wonder.

I am someone you know very well.

I am every man you meet.

I am every woman you meet.

"The Serenity Prayer"

*God grant me the serenity to accept the
things I cannot change,
Courage to change the things I can
and Wisdom to know the difference.*

"Prayer of St. Francis"

*Lord, make me an instrument of Thy peace -
Where there is hatred, I may bring love
Where there is wrong, I may bring spirit of
forgiveness
Where there is discord, I may bring truth
Where there is despair, I may bring hope
Where there are shadows, I may bring light
Where there is sadness, I may bring joy
Lord, grant that I may seek rather to comfort
than to be comforted
To understand, than to be understood
To love, than to be loved
For it is by self - forgetting that one finds
it is by forgiving that one is forgiven.
It is by dying that one awakens to eternal life.*

"Thank God For Today"

This is the beginning of a new day. I can waste it or use it for good. What I do today is important because I am exchanging a day of my life for it.

When tomorrow comes, this day will be gone forever leaving in its place something I have traded for it.

I want it to be gain, not loss; Good, not evil; Success, not failure; In order that I shall not regret the price I paid for today.

-Anonymous

God never gave us a dream without giving us the strength to carry it out.

Fear not tomorrow: God is already there.

"Footprints"

One night a man had a dream. He dreamed he was walking along the beach with the LORD. Across the colorful sky flashed scenes from his life. For each scene, he noticed two sets of footprints; one belonged to him, and the other to the LORD.

When the last scene of his life flashed before him, he looked back at the footprints and noticed that many times along the path of his life there was only one set of footprints. He also noticed that it happened at the very lowest and saddest times in his life.

This really bothered him and he questioned the LORD about it. "LORD, you said that once I decided to believe in you, you'd walk with me all the way. But I have noticed that during the most troublesome times in my life, there is only one set of footprints. I don't understand why when I needed you most you would abandon me."

The LORD said unto him, "My precious, precious child, I love you and would never leave you. During your times of trial and tribulation, when you see only one set of footprints, it was then that I carried you."

-Author Unknown

"The Station"

Tucked away in our subconscious is an idyllic vision. We see ourselves on a long trip that spans the continent. We are traveling by train. Out the windows we drink in the passing scene of cars on nearby highways, of children waving at the crossing, of cattle grazing on a distant hillside; of smoke pouring from a power plant, of row upon row of corn and wheat, of flatlands and valleys, of mountains and rolling hillsides, or city skylines and village halls.

But uppermost in our minds are the final destination. On a certain day at a certain hour we will pull into the station. Bands will be playing and flags waving. Once we get there so many wonderful dreams will come true and the pieces of our lives will fit together like a completed jigsaw puzzle. How restlessly we pace the aisles, damning the minutes for loitering - waiting, waiting for the station.

"When we reach the station, that will be it!" "When I buy a new 450/SL Mercedes Benz!" "When I have paid off the mortgage!" "When I get a promotion!" "When I reach the age of retirement, I shall live happily ever after!"

Sooner or later we must realize there is no station, no one place to arrive at once and for all. The true joy of life is the trip. The station is only a dream. It constantly outdistances us.

"Relish the moment" is a good motto, especially when coupled with Psalms 118:24: *"This is the day which the Lord hath made;we will rejoice and be glad in it."* It isn't the burdens of today that drive men mad. It is the regrets over yesterday and the fear of tomorrow. Regret and fear are twin thieves who rob us of today.

So, stop pacing the aisles and counting the miles. Instead, climb more mountains, eat more ice cream, go barefoot more often, swim more rivers, watch more sunsets, laugh more, cry less. Life must be lived as we go along. The station will come soon enough.

"A Winner's Creed"

If you think you are beaten, you are.
If you think you dare not, you don't.
If you'd like to win, but think you can't,
It's almost a cinch you won't.

If you think you'll lose, you're lost.
For out in the world we find,
Success begins with a person's will.
It's all in the state of mind.

Life's battles don't always go
To the stronger or faster hand,

But sooner or later the person who wins
Is the one who thinks, "I can!"

"Don't Quit"

When things go wrong as they sometimes will,

When the road you're trudging seems all uphill,

When the funds are low and the debts are high

And you want to smile, but you have to sigh,

When care is pressing you down a bit - Rest

if you must,

But Don't You Quit!

Success is failure turned inside out. The

silver tint of the clouds of doubt, And you

never can tell how close you are.

It may be near when it seems afar. So, stick

to the fight when you're hardest hit. It's

when things go wrong that

You Must Not QUIT!

6

Meditations From The Scriptures

*"Prayer cannot mend a broken bridge,
rebuild a ruined city or bring water to
parched fields.
Prayer can mend a broken heart, lift up a
discouraged soul and strengthen a
weakened will."*

Meditations from The Scriptures
Excerpts from The New International Version

Deuteronomy 31:8 *"The Lord himself goes before you and will be with you; he will never leave you nor forsake you. Do not be afraid; do not be discouraged."*

Deuteronomy 33:27a *"The Eternal God is your refuge, and underneath are the everlasting arms."*

Psalms 27:1 *"The Lord is my light and my salvation; whom shall I fear? The Lord is the stronghold of my life; of whom shall I be afraid?"*

Psalm 34:4 *"I sought the Lord, and He answered me; he delivered me from all my fears."*

Psalm 461-2 *"God is our refuge and our strength, a very present help in trouble. Therefore, we will not fear."*

Psalm 112:7 *"He shall not be afraid of evil tidings: his heart is fixed, trusting in the Lord."*

Proverbs 1:33 *"But whoever listens to me will live in safety and be at ease, without fear of harm."*

Proverbs 29:25 *"The fear of man bringeth a snare."*

Isaiah 26:3 *"You will keep in perfect peace him whose mind is steadfast, because he trusts in you."*

Isaiah 35:3-4 *"Strengthen the feeble hands, steady the knees that give way; say to those fearful hearts, Be strong, do not fear;"*

Isaiah 41:10a *"So do not fear, for I am with you; do not be dismayed, for I am your God. I will strengthen you and help you."*

Haggai 2:5 *"According to the word I covenanted with you when ye came out of Egypt, so my spirit remaineth among you: fear ye not."*

John 14:27 *"Peace I leave with you, my peace I give unto you: not as the world giveth, give I unto you. Let not your heart be troubled, neither let it be afraid."*

Romans 8:15 *"For you did not receive a spirit that makes you a slave again to fear, but you received the Spirit of sonship (or adoption)."*

II Timothy 1:7 *"For God did not give us a spirit of timidity (fear), but a spirit of power, of love and of self-discipline."*

Hebrews 2:15 *"And deliver them who through fear of death were all their lifetime subject to bondage."*

Hebrews 13:5-6 *"I will never leave thee nor forsake thee. The Lord is my helper; I will not be afraid. What can man do to me?"*

I Peter 5:7 *"Cast all your anxiety on him because he cares for you."*

I John 4:18 *"There is no fear in love. But perfect love drives out fear, because fear has to do with punishment. The one who fears is not made perfect in love."*

7

Case Studies

"He has not learned the
lesson of life
who does not every day
surmount a fear."

-Ralph Waldo Emerson

MARILYN'S STORY:
A RECOVERING AGORAPHOBIC

In 1976 I had my first panic attack. At that time, I had no idea of what a panic attack was and certainly no idea of what was happening to me.

I had been to the dentist earlier that day and he had given me a shot of novocaine before drilling my tooth. I then met some friends for dinner, where I had a glass of wine and off we went to the movies.

Nothing exceptional was happening in my life and, although there were many stressors in my profession, I was coping quite well.

Then, out of a clear blue sky, about half-way into the film, my hands became cold and clammy, my heart started to race, I became dizzy and nauseous and ran to the ladies room where I threw up. The suddenness and the severity of the attack was so devastating that I grabbed a cab from the theater (not even saying goodbye to my friends) and had him rush me to the nearest emergency room, sure that I was dying. After all emergency screening procedures proved normal, I was released and told to go home and rest.

As soon as I arrived home, I felt better and figured the

novocaine must have reacted with the wine at dinner, and that was the cause of my distress.

I resumed my normal daily activities with no further incidences.

About six months later, once again out of the blue, I had a second attack. This time it was at Disneyland. A friend had some Valium with her so I took a half of a 5 mg. tablet, went to the first aid station, laid down for an hour and felt better. I just wanted to go home.

The next day I felt fine so I easily rationalized my feelings were caused by too much excitement- never seeing a connection between the two isolated incidents.

Then on a Sunday in 1977, I was feeling a little anxious and stressed, so I decided to take a hot bath to help me relax. I crawled into bed to watch "60 Minutes" and started to feel very uneasy, weak, and uncomfortable. My palms started to sweat, I couldn't breathe. I was having hot flashes, chest pains, and heart palpitations. I had this overwhelming feeling of impending doom and was sure that I was having a heart attack.

I was afraid to drive and felt I couldn't wait for a taxi, so I rushed across the street to my neighbor's house and asked her to drive me to the emergency room, where I was promptly admitted with a heart rate of 240 beats per minute. The doctors wanted to admit me to the hospital, but I refused. They kept me there for five hours until my heartbeat returned to normal and sent me home after I promised to see my family physician the following morning. Once I returned home I felt better. I was frightened, but experienced none of the physical and psychological terror of a few hours before so I went to bed and slept quite well.

The following day my doctor, finding nothing wrong with my EKG, diagnosed me as having tachycardia and preventively prescribed Lanoxin (a heart medication). He said I had a bad case of "nerves" and suggested I take a few days off from work and try to relax.

After that Sunday's scare, my panic attacks became more frequent. I started making the rounds of different doctors because I was sure that I was dying and nobody believed me since they could find nothing physically wrong. I had all of the routine lab tests, another EKG, a treadmill test and blood chemistry work-ups. All results were in the normal ranges.

Following my next panic attack, I seriously started doubting my doctor's diagnostic ability, so I made an appointment with the Chief Cardiologist at a neighboring hospital. Once again, he too, found nothing physically wrong.

During one panic attack, my symptoms included dizziness, tingling and numbness of my arms, and this time I was sure that had a brain tumor, so I consulted with a neurologist. This time a whole different set of tests, studies, and scans, with the same results, normal!

My panic attacks were becoming more frequent and my symptoms were not always the same. A month later, when I once again experienced difficulty in breathing and feelings of suffocation, I wound up in the emergency room again and there all procedures again proved normal.

I started listening in to all of my body symptoms and would catastrophize the slightest thing so when I had difficulty swallowing due to a tightness and lump in my throat, I arranged for a consultation with an Eye, Ear, Nose and Throat Specialist. Another false alarm. Still no diagnosis.

One day a friend showed me an article in a women's magazine which described some of my symptoms and attributed them to Hypoglycemia, so off I rushed to an Endocrinologist for an eight hour glucose tolerance test. Same results, normal.

As a last resort, I went to a Gastroenterologist when another well-meaning friend suggested my chest pains might be due to gas. I had an upper G. I. series which also proved normal and with each "normal" finding, I became more and more terrified. I knew something was seriously wrong with me but no doctor could diagnose the problem.

All of my test results were returned to my original family practitioner who told me in no uncertain terms to "pull myself together" and I was nothing more than a hypochondriac and perhaps I should see a psychiatrist and stop wasting his time.

Due to the devastating effects of my unknown illness and the attacks, which were occurring much more frequently, my perimeter was getting smaller and smaller. I became virtually paralyzed with irrational fears. Like the ripples of a stone dropped into a placid pool of water, my circle of fear spread out to encompass all areas of my life. From a creative, personable vibrant, articulate extrovert, I turned into a recluse with millions of excuses as to why I couldn't attend any social functions, go to the market, drive, eat in restaurants, go the movies, etc. I only felt safe and secure at home, where I continually checked my door to make sure the paramedics could get in when called, and lifted the receiver to make sure the phone was working so I could call for help.

My main terror was the thought of mental illness, and now my own trusted physician was confirming my worst fears. Words like madness, insanity, crazy, and lunacy raced through my mind, evoking images of padded cells and straight jackets. I didn't want to live, yet I was too chicken to kill myself, so I reluctantly made an appointment with a psychiatrist. He prescribed anti-depressants, but I rebelled against taking any medication. I had to be in complete control of my life and once I swallowed a pill, I had no control over the effect it would have on me, and I panicked at the thought of the possible side effects. Although I fought taking the medication, I did keep my weekly appointments with my psychiatrist.

It was the blackest summer of my life. Each day my fears and depression worsened. I couldn't sleep. The only time I left my house was to visit the doctor. I couldn't concentrate. I'd try to read something and wound up reading the same sentence over and over again. Even though I had the money, I couldn't pay my bills. Everything was too much of an effort. I had no energy and all I did was cry.

Some people lose weight when they are depressed, others self-medicate with drugs and alcohol. My "drugs" were chocolate, caffeine and nicotine. On the way back from my psychiatrist's office, (which was the only place I went that summer), I traditionally stopped at the market to stock up on ice cream, candy, cigarettes, coffee and dog food. (I had five dogs at the time and if not for them, I wold have committed myself to a mental institution.) I gained forty pounds in two months. In addition to being an emotional basket case, I was a physical wreck as well. I had bottomed out. The only light I could see at the end of the tunnel was an oncoming train, and just wanted to die.

And then it happened. Since, I didn't want to see or be seen by anyone during the day, and couldn't sleep at night, I watered my outside plants in the middle of the night. I don't remember the exact date, but I'll never forget the experience.

On the left side of my house, next to the driveway, I had planted a cactus that a friend had discarded. It was a nightblooming Cereus, and quite ugly and thorny. I never paid much attention to it and left it there since it required a minimum of care and served as a good deterrent to burglars.

On this particular night when I went to water it, I saw on it the most magnificent flower I had ever seen. I couldn't believe my eyes. This cactus that had never bloomed in the ten years I had it, amidst its ugliness and thorns, produced a flower that was complete perfection. I get chills even as I write this, because that cactus, which we have chosen for the cover of this book, was the turning point in my life. When I saw such beauty could be produced and emerge from such ugliness, I realized from my deep despair something, too, might be able to flourish. I cried that night as I have never cried before and then a calmness followed.

The next morning, I called a trusted friend and asked him to come over and sit with me while I took the medication my psychiatrist had prescribed six months ago that lay untouched in the medicine cabinet. I then made an appointment with my Rabbi to discuss my "condition", ask for his advice, and tell him about the "miracle" which had occurred in my life.

I have never been devoutly religious, but this cactus blooming, to me, was a sign - a spiritual awakening. I was no longer alone - there was a Higher Power. I just had to acknowledge it and let it in.

Even though I still didn't know what was wrong with me, the medication was beginning to lift my depression and block some of my anxiety. I became semi-functional and was able to return to work, but I still existed in a state of anticipatory anxiety - not knowing when, where, or if the next attack would occur. I continued to avoid all other common places and activities.

Then another unexpected and unexplained development occurred. While watching television one night, I saw a program with an agoraphobic as its main character and it was me! All my symptoms - all my fears - all my anxiety - were portrayed on the screen and I finally had a name for my "condition". I wasn't alone! I wasn't going crazy. What I had was agoraphobia! My self-diagnosis in itself was therapeutic and offered my first ray of hope for potential recovery.

Life at its best is not easy, but I found that as soon as I gave up trying to control my life, the pieces started to fit together like a well-made puzzle, and things started falling into place.

1. I suffered from the devastation of Agoraphobia (acute anxiety and panic attacks) and vowed if I ever became functional again. I would dedicate my life to helping others with this problem. This gave birth to the Institute for Phobic Awareness.

2. Upon my return from Workman's Compensation leave, I was assigned to teach at a residential drug and alcohol recovery center in Desert Hot Springs. It was there that I was introduced to the Twelve Step program of A. A. that I saw used so successfully in the recovery process of my students. This contributed to Rosemary and myself starting a Phobics Anonymous group which eventually led us to the authorship of this text.

3. In 1985, Rosemary, a suffering social phobic (who was also affiliated with Al-Anon Twelve Step program), joined the Institute for Phobic Awareness. She became the spiritual component of our group and suggested

we adopt the 12 steps to phobias and panic attacks. Through our affiliation we decided to add a Twelve Step program for phobics in addition to the ongoing support groups already in existence. This commenced Phobics Anonymous.

HISTORY OF PHOBICS ANONYMOUS

Phobics Anonymous was formed as a 12 Step Recovery program and fellowship in 1989. It grew out of the personal experience of two women who had suffered from panic attacks and phobias and who were willing to share their experience, strength and hope in recovery, thereby helping others who suffer. Both women, Marilyn and Rosemary, were friends, teachers and colleagues. Both served as channels for a Higher Power or God, as one understands Him, by sharing their experience, strength and hope.

Marilyn, seeking to further the knowledge and education of those who suffer from panic attacks, established in 1981 The Institute for Phobic Awareness. Through this Institute, she brought resources and awareness to the public through speaking, writing, offering individual therapeutic help and through a self-help group.

Rosemary sought out help for her social phobia and panic attacks in 1985 when she attended the Institute's self-help group. Rosemary had also been attending a 12 Step fellowship of Al Anon.

Rosemary, seeing in Al Anon how wonderful the spiritual approach to recovery is, suggested to Marilyn the idea to adapt the 12 Steps to people recovering from phobias and panic attacks, in addition to the already existing resources. Both Marilyn and Rosemary felt inspired to proceed and apply the 12 Steps to phobias and panic disorders. Thus was the beginning of Phobics Anonymous.

Rosemary wrote the 12 Step portion of their book *The Twelve Steps of Phobics Anonymous* at a spiritual retreat She and Marilyn collaborated together and wrote the remainder of the book. Marilyn invested her time, work, and finances, having the Institute for Phobic Awareness publish their work in 1989.

Phobics Anonymous meetings were begun. Phobics Anonymous is standing the test of time for the last 27 years and is learning and modifying areas in its growth process of establishing its 12 Steps and 12 Traditions. Birthing and growing pains have been experienced but through the grace and guidance of a Higher Power, Phobics Anonymous is bearing fruit. For this we give our Higher Power Thanks!

ROSEMARY'S STORY:
A RECOVERING SOCIAL PHOBIC

To all the suffering social phobics, I desire my story will give you hope.

To tell my story is to tell a journey. Some is happy. Some is sad. Some is heartbreaking. Some is very difficult. But it is a story of victory over fear.

When I was a young girl, I experienced the joyful spontaneity of youth - the laughter, the running in the breeze, the freedom. At sixteen, I became sexually involved with my boyfriend. I did not want to lose him.

My first panic attack happened when I saw him talking with two other teenage girls. Fear and panic gripped my heart. Was he rejecting me, abandoning me?

My panic attacks spread to many other situations involving being with people, especially boys, men, and authority figures. My particular panic attack involved intense fear, pounding heart, sweating palms, a paralysis of facial muscles, feeling like I couldn't smile, and a lack of spontaneity. The panic built up to such an intense peak I felt totally out of control, unable to function, to smile, to carry on a conversation. I doubted whether I'd know my own name if asked. The feeling was so intense I became afraid of the fear itself. I thought I was afraid of people, but I was really afraid of the panic attacks. I did not want to experience this horrible feeling, plus, it was very embarrassing. I certainly did not want others to see I was afraid. I felt very badly for the other people and how they must feel, thinking I was so very afraid of them. I felt totally inadequate to deal with these attacks.

My way to deal with the attacks was to avoid as much as possible any people or situations in which I would get panicky. Thus began the self-imposed prison process. The range of activities I participated in became more narrow.

I really could not date other fellows easily. The panic attacks would ruin any enjoyment from the experience. I became more and more dependent on my boyfriend. After going steady for three years, we were married. I felt very comfortable and safe with him. I loved him very much but now know I put my burden of fear onto him. I depended on him for my happiness, an unfair assumption.

My social phobia became very pronounced. The symptoms were under control in my family and my safe circle of friends. But give me anything to do in front of a group, or a job interview, and I would panic.

I sought medical help through psychologists, counselors, family doctors, books. I read whatever I could get my hands on. I prayed.

Throughout these years, I found it extremely painful and anxiety provoking to interact with people on an intimate level, especially men and authority figures.

After sixteen years of this phobic avoidant behavior, a friend gave me some Valium, which was a very popular medication in the 70's. The Valium was so effective at relieving my panic symptoms I felt normal again. It had been years since I could interact comfortably with people and groups. I had always been frightened to participate in a small group where I might have had to read or share orally.

The freedom I felt from the Valium allowed me to engage in social interactions I would have never participated in before. Unfortunately, I abused this new-found, so called freedom. I was disenchanted with my marriage. With my social fear anesthetized by Valium, I ventured into unacceptable adulterous behavior. I soon discovered that a Valium and a drink really smoothed the edge. I could be relaxed, spontaneous, unafraid. What I failed to realize was this was a fraud. Take away the tranquilizer and the alcohol, and I was just as panic stricken as before. The sense of freedom experienced from these chemicals was false. In defense of the newest anti-anxiety, panic blocking agents, I do see a constructive use for medication in controlled moderation to help the phobic enter a feared situation, but the medication itself does not offer permanent freedom. It can, in addictive personalities, lead to chemical dependency and often the throes of addiction.

To my regret and shame, I misused this chemically induced freedom to enter into a promiscuous time of my life with a lot of interaction in dating. It was like making up for lost time. Needless to say, this contributed to a divorce after 18 years of marriage and three children. I consider the following six years as being in the pit. I entered four subsequent marriages during this time. I moved no less than 15 times. My interpersonal relations were based on fear. I was afraid to be alone.

During this time, I was introduced to the Twelve Steps, having married a very ill, active alcoholic. In sheer desperation, I took myself to an Al-Anon meeting. I began to work the Twelve Steps. I saw my own phobic behavior more clearly and began recovery in a self-help group sponsored by the Institute for Phobic Awareness. The love, support, and friendship of this group of fellow-suffering phobics made me realize I was not alone. They were always there if I needed them.

Through six years of applying the Twelve Steps to my phobias and panic attacks, I began recovery. My Higher Power, who I choose to call Jesus, began to deliver me from my fears. Day by day, one step at a time, I began to know who I really am, a child of God, worthwhile and valuable.

I had to "bottom out", experience severe losses; husbands, children, home, and to completely surrender to my Higher Power. He met me at my point of need. He began to lift me up, to heal my wounds, to give me a new life. As Step Twelve says, I had a spiritual experience that clearly revealed to me the love and power of my Higher Power and His continual close presence in my life. This I could never deny.

My spiritual experience which I now refer to as "the gift of a glimpse of the Glory of God" occurred one evening while I was lying in bed recovering from a bad bout with the flu. I had been sick with the flu and bronchitis. Every part of my body ached, especially my chest from so much coughing. Physically, I felt terrible.

Emotionally, I was in the pit. My first and second marriages had failed. I was renting a two bedroom apartment with my three children sleeping in one room. I had lost my home. Needless to say my depression was at a very low point.

I felt deserted, abandoned, sick, alone, and despairing.

My children were not at home. I felt too weak to even go the kitchen and get some soup.

I laid there and said a prayer. I felt alone, sad, and forsaken.

It was a very real experience. I felt a rush of heat or warm energy go from my feet, up my legs, through my body, and into my hands. My hands felt especially warm, even hot. As this warmth filled me, I lost all physical pain - my chest did not hurt nor did my body ache. I felt light - totally physically painless!

In addition to the release of physical pain, I lost all emotional despair. I felt totally peaceful and serene.

At this point I felt a completely real, and unique presence on the upper left side of my room - not a visible form but an acute awareness of a presence. I had an intense feeling of the glory, beauty, brilliance, and especially power right near me. The words I can use to describe this presence are extreme glory, love, peace, beauty, and absolute nearness. Most apparent to me was the power of this presence - extremely loving but very powerful and glorious.

The main message I received was that this power or presence was right here with me, not something distant and far away, the great "I Am".

I knew I was not alone. I knew there was a reality more real than the physical and emotional pain I had been feeling. I knew this reality was not far away.

With this profound revelation, the warmth left my physical body and my hands became normal temperature again. I returned to my former state but without as much physical and emotional pain. I was overjoyed at what I term, a "glimpse through the veil."

My daughter came home and into my room. All I could say to her was "Do not worry about what happens to you in this physical realm". "You're never alone. There's a reality more real and powerful than this, and it's right with you all the time."

What I really felt after that experience, was that our material world is the illusion, and what I had experienced, a gift to me, is the ultimate reality. I'm thankful for this gift and knowledge.

It is through The Twelve Steps of Phobics Anonymous that I came to know freedom from fear. To me, it is a gift from my Higher Power. My worth and value are no longer dependent on what others think of me. My Higher Power loves me. My guilt of poor choices and poor behavior is absolved.

I define my Higher Power, who I call Jesus, as absolute love, goodness, holiness. He is kind, forgiving, compassionate, wise and just. This Higher Power is the Alpha and Omega who transcends time and space, who heals our pain, redeems us. He is Glorious, Sovereign and Powerful. I give Him thanks and praise. He is right here, and I receive Him again today, as I do each day.

Learning to live a new life of freedom, joy, peace and gratitude comes one day at a time. When relapses occur of falling into negative, fearful thinking, I turn to my Higher Power and I persevere.

I now greet people with calm serenity. I participate without fear in small groups. I lead small group meetings. I look forward to interacting with people. I no longer avoid contacts. My Higher Power has given me new life. With this new life, I am not motivated by fear but by love. Through the grace of God, I try not to compromise my new freedom in any way. It is a time for me to stand fast in this new liberty and to reach out to others in love.

My continual prayer in my ongoing spiritual growth and sanctification process is defined in the following anonymous saying.

"Oh, empty us of self, selfishness, the world, and sin,
And then in all Thy fullness enter in;
Take full possession Lord, and let each thought
Into obedience unto thee be brought;
Thine is the power, and Thine, the will that we be wholly
sanctified, oh Lord, to Thee"

Philippians 4:6 *"Do not be anxious about anything, but in everything, by prayer and petition with thanksgiving, present your requests to God. And the peace of God, which transcends all understanding, will guard your heart and your mind through Christ Jesus."*

John 17:22-23 *"And the Glory which you gave Me, I have given them…I in them and You in Me…and that the world may know that You have sent Me, and have loved them as You have loved Me."*

8

The Relationship Between Substance Abuse, Addiction, and Anxiety Disorders

"Wine drunk with an equal quantity of

water puts away anxiety and terrors".

- Hippocrates "Aphorism"

There appear to be consistent, scientific findings recently which prove persons suffering from anxiety and panic-related disorders are prone to the development of concurrent problems of substance abuse. Use and frequent abuse of sedatives and alcohol in an effort to self-medicate and reduce anticipatory anxiety, allow the user to cope with phobic anxiety and prevent panic.

Psychoactive drugs are drugs which effect the central nervous system. They produce a false sense of well-being and bring relief from tension, anxiety, and fear.

Alcohol is a drug with ethyl alcohol as its main ingredient. It is one of the most widely used and abused of the psychoactive drugs. Just a small amount effects the cerebral cortex, the part of the brain that controls thoughts, judgment and self-control. By suppressing these functions, psychoactive drugs produce feelings of relaxation and freedom from fear.

A higher concentration slows the brain centers governing speech, vision, hearing, coordination, and balance. As a result, the user may experience slurred speech, double vision, and staggering, the same symptoms associated with panic attacks.

This form of self-medication or tension reduction is

often used to enable the phobic to accomplish necessary activities, including work or school requirements, to venture into public without fear of social rejection, to cope with the anticipation of panic attacks, and phobic anxiety. It increases risk-taking, has been found to decrease memory for unpleasant feelings, and reduce catastrophic thinking.

Anxiety and panic-related disorders often start during periods of high stress or trauma and heavy chemical use is also used as a response to periods of stress. Many drink or use drugs to "feel normal" and adjust their level of usage in accordance with their level of anxiety. Therefore, it has been speculated those suffering from anxiety and panic-related disorders might use alcohol or drugs to the point of addiction in a mistaken attempt to prevent panic. It's interesting to note many of the chemicals used are not pharmacologically effective anti-anxiety agents. They may even increase panic by contributing to the loss of control and the dreaded body symptoms leading to catastrophic misinterpretation of them which, in itself, leads to panic.

Data from the National Institute of Mental Health showed that four major disorders commonly begin in late adolescence or young adulthood. The median age at onset for anxiety disorders is 15 years; for major depressive episodes, 24 years; for drug abuse or dependence, 19 years; and for alcohol abuse or dependence, 21 years.

Findings also suggest for persons 18-30 years old, having a major depressive episode or anxiety disorder double the risk for later chemical abuse dependence or addiction.

There also seems to be the same familiar propensity for a lifetime history of chemical abuse and anxiety disorders. Within families of those suffering from anxiety disorders, parental alcoholism is seen more frequently than would be expected by chance. This prevalence and the co-occurrence of anxiety disorders and alcoholism in individual families and the general population has been documented and cannot be ignored since specific treatment of the mood or anxiety disorder may reduce substance abuse as well.

Recent finding also show persons leaving recovery centers after detoxification are experiencing spontaneous panic attacks for the first time in their lives and so begins a vicious cycle.

Consider the following statements to see if you are using chemicals to help alleviate or manage your anxiety.

1. The best thing about the use of chemicals is I feel less afraid, anxious, and more relaxed.

2. I use chemicals not so much for enjoyment but to make me feel and act "normal".

3. On days I feel less anxious, I use less alcohol or drugs.

Then on stressful days when I feel more anxious and tense, they help take the "edge off".

4. Using drugs or alcohol prevents my having catastrophic, frightening, or anxiety-provoking thoughts.

5. Sometimes I need drugs or alcohol to stop the feelings I'm going to die or lose control.

6. I use chemicals before venturing into social situations or going out in public.

7. I avoid social situations or restaurants where no alcohol or drugs are available.

8. The use of chemicals help me get through the day and accomplish things I need to get done.

9. If not for alcohol or drugs, I wouldn't be able to tolerate my job or school.

10. I drank or used drugs to excess before I started having panic attacks.

11. When I try to stop using or abusing chemicals, I experience spontaneous panic attacks I never had before.

One thing about alcohol, it works. It may destroy mans' career, ruin his marriage, turn him into a zombie unconscious in a hallway- but it works. On short term, it works much faster than a psychiatrist, or a priest, or the love of a husband or a wife.

Those things... They all take time. They must be developed... But alcohol is always ready to go to work at once. Within minutes, the little formless fears are gone or turned into harmless amusement. But they come back, oh yes, and they bring reinforcements.

From "Carlotta McBride" a fictional study of an alcoholic by Charles Orson Gorman.

MARY ANN'S STORY:
TWELVE STEPS TO SERENITY

It was the night after Thanksgiving 1979, I was drunk, and had ruined another family gathering. For over twenty years I had used and abused alcohol to relieve my panic attacks. Now it had become my enemy. I was an alcoholic, and drinking no longer helped. Alcohol began triggering anger. I would verbally lash out at my family. That night my husband of thirty-one years informed me I must do some thing about my drinking and behavior or he would.

I went to bed in the spare room and hugged the large towel I needed for night sweats. The shock of my husband's ultimatum had sobered me, and I was in a state of incredible terror. It was not the irrational fear of a panic attack. I was scared to death and realized I had to act first if I didn't want to find out what he had in mind!

In the morning I had the usual hangover, and my fear was so overwhelming I prayed to die. To this day I don't know how or why I decided to call Alcoholics Anonymous, since it had never crossed my mind before. When I placed the call, I almost hung up, but a friendly voice answered, and I agreed to go to a meeting that night. I hung up and immediately started plotting how I could avoid going, but my anxiety subsided, and I didn't feel the need to drink all day. Miraculously I attended my first A. A. meeting cold sober, and I have not had a drink since.

In spite of my panic and anxiety I felt compelled to attend meetings. It took a long time for me to comprehend the reading of "How it works" at every meeting. What were those steps and slogans all about? How could I ever stop projecting and "Live one day at a time"? I couldn't possible "Let go and let God" or "Turn my will and my life over to the care of God." I finally realized I had done just that when I placed the call to A. A. The third step prayer says, "Relieve me of the bondage of self." I had been a prisoner of my own thinking for so long I couldn't imagine freedom from panic and anxiety. I wasn't even sure I could handle it, but as I worked my way through the steps and became more involved in A. A., I found myself doing many things I had avoided for years. I was driving myself to meetings and picking up others. Doing Twelve Step work and being on the answering service made me realize helping others took my mind off of me. "The Serenity Prayer" replaced my "Stinking Thinking". What an appropriate term that is!

I went to A. A. to stop drinking, and I was given a whole new way of life by the grace of God. The Twelve Step Program works in many wonderful ways. We celebrated our Forty-Second Wedding Anniversary on January 31, 1990.

Serenity Prayer

God grant me the serenity to accept the

things I cannot change.

(The way God made me!)

The courage to change the things I can.

(My thinking!)

The wisdom to know the difference.

(Amen)

LORNA'S STORY

I'm not sure I remember my very first panic attack but one of the first I remember happened while I was in the cafeteria line at the hospital where I worked. For no apparent reason, my heart started racing, I felt as though I could not breathe and by the time I was paying the cashier for my lunch, I was shaking and felt I was going to faint.

By the time this incident took place, I had spent ten years or so abusing alcohol and other drugs off and on- mostly on. In my early 20's, I was "coming out" in the gay and lesbian world and going to the gay bars. I was what I considered a "social drinker and user". Drinking, smoking marijuana, and taking an occasional upper or downer was reserved primarily for the weekends to help me feel more outgoing and comfortable since I had always been rather introverted.

When I was about 23 I began having problems with hyperventilation and was put on tranquilizers. Around that same time I ended up in a psychiatric hospital for severe depression. When I left the hospital after six weeks, I was on seven different kinds of drugs. My drinking and drug use increased rapidly. My life then is much of a blur. I know I moved around a lot, worked very little, and began to develop intestinal problems. I did not attribute any of my problems, whether they be physical or emotional, to alcohol or drugs.

In 1975 I entered into my first of several relationships with other women who basically took care of me. Although I worked, I often had to do things I either didn't like to do or felt uncomfortable doing. My drinking and using was somewhat controlled by them until they realized they could not change my character defects. This always brought an end to the relationship which would catapult me into months of serious drinking and using to make up for the time I had lost while in a relationship.

I somehow found the courage (most likely from my chemicals) to become actively involved in the gay and lesbian political community. My leadership role required me to be in the forefront quite often and I normally self-medicated myself enough to decrease my anxiety. When my self-medication via alcohol began to cause black-outs for me at political functions, I summoned the will to stop drinking. However, I did not give up others drugs and often dealt with my anxiety with tranquilizers or marijuana.

About a year and a half later I began drinking again. It was worse than ever and shortly thereafter I went bankrupt, lost my apartment and moved to the desert to begin a new job and try to get myself together.

While my drinking and drug intake increased, so did my panic attacks. Soon I was avoiding grocery stores, theaters, and other places where there were lines or crowds. Whenever I was going out somewhere where there would be a lot of people, I drank before leaving home.

In July of 1986 I finally hit my bottom and entered an outpatient chemical dependency treatment program and began attending Alcoholics Anonymous meetings regularly. I got into a relationship with another recovering alcoholic and my life finally seemed to be coming together - except for one thing. My panic attacks began to rapidly increase in frequency and severity.

I found I could not go to the market alone. At work I started going to lunch early enough to avoid crowds in the cafeteria and finally stopped going there altogether since I was unable to go without experiencing the panic and disorientation. I began to have occasional attacks at A. A. meetings and while I was driving. I had to drive in the right hand lane in case I would have to pull over quickly.

I was terrified the day I unexpectedly had a panic attack at my desk while working. A friend had to drive me home. My world was getting smaller and smaller and I no longer had the "luxury" of self-medicating myself with alcohol and drugs.

One night while driving home from an A. A. meeting that I felt the need to leave, I began to think going back to drinking would be easier than dealing with the panic. This was two and a half years after my last drink.

I sought help through therapy until my therapist suggested tranquilizers to me. I found a psychiatrist who worked in the field of chemical dependency and was convinced to go on a non-addicting drug used with phobics. He had diagnosed me as agoraphobic. Although the medication brought me some relief, I was still subjected to the panic a few times a week and I still avoided markets, the cafeteria and all lines.

In addition to the medication, I was referred to a therapist who worked with me through such things as relaxation exercises and desensitization. She also encouraged me to attend Phobics Anonymous meetings since I felt I had no one in my life who could really understand what I was going through. Phobics Anonymous is based on the Twelve Steps as in A. A. I felt it could help me as A. A. had helped me with my sobriety and my relationship with a Higher Power.

In many ways, this has been a more difficult disorder for me to deal with than my chemical dependency but finding Phobics Anonymous and recovering phobics has contributed to my sense of hope for my own recovery. I am grateful for this.

9

How to Conduct a
Twelve Step Meeting

This chapter will present a format for conducting a Phobics Anonymous meeting. We have found one or two hours is an adequate length of time for constructive interaction. Meetings should be held at least once a week if possible. The meeting has a leader who is a member of the group. Each week leadership changes on a voluntary basis.

The group leader introduces herself or himself and reads the Welcome. Members are invited to participate freely or to just listen and to accept or reject what they like. The meeting format is located in a small spiral notebook. Each week it is available to the new facilitator.

One member is voluntarily asked to read the Description of the Phobic. Another is asked to read the Twelve Steps and a third is asked to read the Promises.

After the initial readings, each member introduces himself by first name only. Each person is orally greeted by the rest of the group.

The leader takes three to five minutes to share his or her own story, to share his experience, strength, and hope. After the leader shares, group members are reminded to keep their individual sharing at a courteous time level not more than three or four minutes. Members are encouraged to keep their sharing as positive and uplifting as possible.

Yet all are free to share any crisis, tears, or pain which is felt. The members of the group encourage one another in love, compassion, guidance, and validation. (All sharing is to be kept confidential).

The group leader can then pick a topic for discussion. It can be one of the steps or it can be a theme;such as, honesty, powerlessness, denial, etc.

The leader opens the floor to any newcomer or person in crisis who needs immediate help. After that, the leader turns over the discussion to anyone who would like to share. Participation is strictly voluntary.

A basket is passed for voluntary contribution. The leader asks for a volunteer to lead the following week's meeting.

The meeting is closed with the group forming a circle, holding hands, and someone leading a closing prayer of choice.

Refreshments are available and members receive a telephone list to use for ongoing support contact. Phobics Anonymous literature is displayed.

The non-threatening, supportive, small group concept of people helping people works well with phobics. We found we could identify with each other. We found by sharing and caring, we were not alone. We began to recover. We felt the help of our Higher Power work through each other in the group in love, support, and guidance.

Following is the Welcome read at the beginning of the meeting.

THE WELCOME

We welcome you to our Phobic Anonymous meeting. We are a group of people who share the common denominator of irrational fears or phobias accompanied by acute panic attacks. We are here to share our experience, strength, and hope.

Through following *The Twelve Steps of Phobics Anonymous*, we are on a journey to wholeness, wellness, and a life based on faith not fear.

We are pleased you are here. We ask that you come here with an open mind and a willingness. Take what you want from our group dialogue and leave the rest. Please respect the confidentiality and anonymity of what's said in this room as we share and grow together in the unity of the Spirit.

DESCRIPTION OF THE PHOBIC
Who is a Phobic?

We are a group of individuals who found that we are powerless over fear. We experience irrational fears often accompanied by acute anxiety and panic attacks. At times we experienced the following physical symptoms to such an extent that they made our lives unmanageable.

Our fear of fear - of being trapped in our emotions, made us feel we were either going crazy, going to lose control, or die. The perimeter of our world became smaller and smaller as we avoided situations, people, and places; such as markets, restaurants, theaters, social functions, driving, job related activities, etc.

We sought help from physicians, psychologists, psychiatrists, hypnotherapists, nutritionists, family, and friends. Many of us self-medicated with alcohol and drugs. All of these provided temporary relief. They addressed the physical, emotional, and intellectual part of man. Yet, there was a missing link. We found the recovery process was incomplete without addressing the spiritual aspect of man.

The Twelve Steps of Phobics Anonymous

1. We admitted that we were powerless over Fear - that our lives had become unmanageable.

2. Came to believe that a power greater than ourselves could restore us to wholeness.

3. Made a decision to turn our will and our lives over to the care of God, <u>as we understood our Him</u>.

4. Made a searching and fearless moral inventory of ourselves.

5. Admitted to our God, to ourselves, and to another human being the exact nature of our wrongs.

6. Were entirely ready to have our God remove all these defects of character.

7. Humbly asked Him to remove our shortcomings.

8. Made a list of all persons we had harmed, and became willing to make amends to them all.

9. Made direct amends to such people wherever possible, except when to do so would injure them or others.

10. Continued to take a daily inventory and when we were wrong, promptly admitted it.

11. Sought through prayer and meditation to improve our conscious contact with God <u>as we understood Him</u>, praying only for knowledge of His will for us and the power to carry that out.

12. Having had a spiritual awakening as the result of these steps, we tried to carry this message to others, and to practice these principles in all our affairs.

The Twelve Traditions of Phobics Anonymous

1. Our common welfare should come first; personal recovery depends upon PA unity.

2. For our group purpose there is but one ultimate authority - a loving God as He may express Himself in our group conscience. Our leaders are but trusted servants, they do not govern.

3. The only requirement for membership is a desire to recover from phobias and panic attacks.

4. Each group should be autonomous except in matters affecting other groups or PA as a whole.

5. Each group has but one primary purpose - to carry the message to the phobic who still suffers.

6. A PA group ought never endorse, finance, or lend the PA name to any related facility or outside enterprise, lest problems of money, property or prestige divert us from our primary spiritual purpose.

7. Every PA group ought to be fully self-supporting, declining outside contributions.

8. Phobics Anonymous should remain forever nonprofessional, but our service centers may employ special workers.

9. PA, as such, ought never be organized, but may create service boards or committees directly responsible to those they serve.

10. Phobics Anonymous has no opinion on outside issues; hence the PA name ought never be drawn into public controversy.

11. Our public relations policy is based on attraction rather than promotion; we need always maintain personal anonymity at the level of press, radio, and films.

12. Anonymity is the spiritual foundation of all our Traditions, ever reminding us to place principles before personalities.

The Promises

- Recovery is an ongoing daily process which requires commitment and dedication leading to continuous progress and growth.

- We will be amazed before we are half-way through.

- We are going to experience a feeling of freedom and newly found happiness.

- We will not regret the past nor wish to shut the door on it but will use our painful experience as a stepping stone for growth.

- We will comprehend the word serenity, and we will experience calmness and freedom from fear.

- No matter how high on the anxiety scale our fear has peaked, we will see how our experience can benefit others, and in helping them we will aid our own recovery.

- We will no longer fear nor be anxious about how others respond to our feelings. Our need to be perfectionistic and people-pleasers will diminish.

- We will no longer fear rejections nor being hurt by others.

- We will no longer respond in fear to other peoples' actions and attitudes.

- What we say and how we act will no longer be determined by our fear of others' feelings.

- We will no longer have difficulty expressing our feelings.

- Our serenity will no longer be determined by how others are feeling or behaving.

- The feelings of uselessness, rejection, abandonment, and self-pity will disappear.

- We will no longer be the nucleus of our own world but will gain an interest and understanding of our fellow phobics.

- Our self-will and compulsion for control will leave us.

- Our catastrophic and negative thinking as well as our attitudes will change.

- Fear of people, places, things, and situations will be replaced by faith.

- We will learn how to accept, cope with, and float through situations which previously panicked us.

- We will come to accept our Higher Power and realize our Higher Power is doing for us what we could not do for ourselves.

- We will gain the inner direction to stand and face our fears rather than retreat.

- Our shame, bondage, and self-made prison walls will crumble.

Appendix

Definition of Terms

Agoraphobia:

A complex set of fears and avoidance behaviors marked by anxiety, panic attacks, and losing control. Lifestyle can be severely limited.

The term agoraphobia is derived from the Greek words "agora" meaning "a place of assembly" and "phobos", meaning "flight - panic". The word agoraphobia was first used by Westphal in 1871.

Agoraphobia is sometimes referred to as fear of open spaces or fear of the market place. I chose to more accurately define it from my own personal experience as a fear of the fear reaction. A condition in which a person suffers such incapacitating, debilitating, paralyzing, confusing, intense fear so terrifying, its victim lives in constant fear of repeating the experience which first triggered the reaction or panic attack. Like the ripples of a stone dropped into a placid pool of water, the circles of fear spread out until they encompass the marketplace, the street, the vehicles, and conveyances of ordinary life and indeed everything beyond the agoraphobic's front door.

It is not the fear of a specific place which holds us prisoner under house arrest. It is the fear of having another panic attack and being caught, trapped, or unable to run away, and seek help if that panic attack should occur again.

Agoraphobia, as I shall use the term differs fundamentally and significantly from monosymptomatic phobias such as fear of spiders, death, germs, etc. The person with a specific phobia is afraid of an object outside himself. The agoraphobic fears situations but not quite in the same way. He fears the feelings which arise within himself during a panic attack. The bottom line being, he will lose control, go crazy, or die.

Anticipatory Anxiety (or the "What if…" Syndrome):

This type of anxiety comes on in anticipation. "What if I get panicky when I go into a situation?" The "What if…" intensity of this anxiety increases gradually. It does not have the extreme, bizarre, and terrifying symptoms spontaneous anxiety attacks do. Many "normal" people have some anticipatory anxiety before going on a stage, making a speech, etc.

Anxiety:

A vague fear, a sense of helpless foreboding which is not directed toward the here and now.

The American Psychiatric Association defines it as "apprehension, tension, or uneasiness that stems from the anticipation of danger, the course of which is largely unknown, or unverbalized." Anxiety is not always unhealthy even when it covers a whole spectrum of distant possibilities. However, one abnormal state is chronic anxiety which is often described as free floating or generalized rather than being specifically anchored to one set of objects or one situation. Anxiety is also abnormal when it is not based on reality- what really could happen- or when it inhibits our daily activities.

The Anxiety Scale:

Symptoms are placed in a scale from 1 to 10 for the convenience of discussing the severity of the anxiety without "symptom swapping" which can be contagious.

THE ANXIETY SCALE
Functional

1. "Butterflies", a queasy feeling in stomach, trembling, jitteriness, tension.

2. Cold or clammy palms, hot flashes and warm all over, profuse sweating.

3. Very rapid, strong, racing, pounding or irregular heartbeat, tremors, muscle tension and aches, fatigue.

Decreased Functional Ability

4. Jelly legs, wobbly, weak in knees, unsteady feelings, shakiness.

5. Immediate desperate and urgent need to escape, avoid or hide.

6. Lump in throat, dry mouth, choking, muscle tension.

7. Hyperventilation, tightness in chest, shortness of breath, smothering sensation.

Very Limited or Completely Non-Functional

8. Feelings of impending doom or death, high pulse rate, difficulty breathing, palpitations.

9. Dizziness, visual distortion, faintness, headache, nausea, numbness, tingling of hands, feet or other body parts, diarrhea, frequent urination.

10. COMPLETE PANIC, non-functional, disoriented, detached, feelings of unreality, paralyzed, fear of dying, going crazy, or losing control.*

Frequently people experiencing their first spontaneous "panic attack", rush to emergency rooms convinced that they are having a heart attack.

Endogenous Anxiety:

"Endogenous" comes from the Greek word meaning "to

be born or produced from within". The latest research shows this condition is a disease whose victims appear to be born with a genetic vulnerability to it. In this anxiety disease, like other diseases, nature has malfunctioned in some way, and like other diseases, it has a life of its own and brings misery and suffering.

Exogenous Anxiety:

"Exogenous" comes from the Greek word meaning "to be born or produced from the outside". It is an ordinary defensive reaction to a justifiable source.

Fear:

A basic emotional response to a specific situation or to an imagined threat. It's a reaction probably both inborn and learned. It is a protective response much like pain and like pain, can be most uncomfortable. Fear is nature's way of alerting us to danger and protecting us from harm. We need a healthy fear of cars for instance so we won't cross the street carelessly. It doesn't mean we should be so frightened of them we won't cross the street at all. Such a persistent fear is an irrational fear.

Irrational Fear:

A persistent, unexplained fear which disrupts our lives and consumes a tremendous amount of emotional energy without providing any benefit.

Panic:

Sudden burst of abrupt and uncontrollable, unmanageable terror usually in the face of an immediate threat either real or imagined resulting in the fight or flight syndrome.

Panic Attack:

May be used interchangeably with the term acute anxiety attacks. Bodily symptoms are the same.

Panic Disorder:

A psychological problem whose predominant symptom is recurring panic attacks.

Phobia:

An involuntary fear reaction inappropriate to the situation. It involves a sense of dread so intense the person either does everything possible to avoid it, or experiences extreme discomfort while enduring the source of distress.

Safe Place:

An agoraphobic's "safe place" is their area of security. In the course of events when a phobic returns to their "safe place" the panic subsides. For most agoraphobics, it is usually the home. Once this area is established, any attempts to exceed its boundaries may bring anxiety and if you venture too far there will be panic.

Setbacks:

Old habits are not easy to break even when they are bad habits. Therefore, for some unknown reason after doing something successfully you may have a setback and revert back to your old maladaptive habit patterns.

Simple Phobia:

Characterized by dread and avoidance of a specific object or situation, such as highway driving, heights, snakes, and closed-in places.

Social Phobia:

An extreme anxiety and panic in social situations, fearing some particular action will be noticed by others, one will be judged by others, and behave in a way leading to extreme embarrassment. Examples are public speaking, eating in public, and dating.

Spontaneous Anxiety Attacks or Panic:

The anxiety surges suddenly, unexpectedly, and for no apparent reason. It seems to overwhelm and panic the body before the mind can fully figure out how to cope with it. It rushes to peak intensity (a "10" - see anxiety scale) very quickly.

When these two companions, the spontaneous attacks and the anticipatory episodes join forces the victim crosses a threshold into a new realm of progressive disability.

Support Person or Sponsor:

A trusted, recovering, non-judgmental fellow phobic who can be turned to in time of need for assistance, encouragement, and guidance.

> *We all need a helping hand.*
>
> *Someone to share with,*
>
> *who will understand.*
>
> *Special people to see us through,*
>
> *the glad times and the sad times too.*
>
> *A sponsor on whom we can always depend.*
>
> *A support person we can call a friend.*

Symptom Swapping:

This can be a major problem within groups. It happens when a person who is highly verbal and descriptive relates their symptoms and after listening to them, you acquire them. Using only the numbers on the anxiety scale to describe feelings provides an insulation from this phenomena.

The Twelve Steps of
Phobics Anonymous

Paperback and kindle versions available at amazon.com

Please find more books by Rosemary on amazon.com, available in paperback and kindle.

One Day at a Time in Phobics Victorious
The Twelve Steps of Phobics Victorious
Jesus, My Higher Power

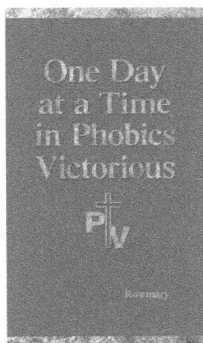

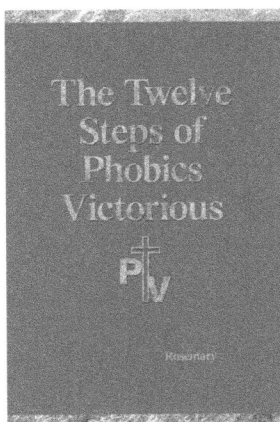

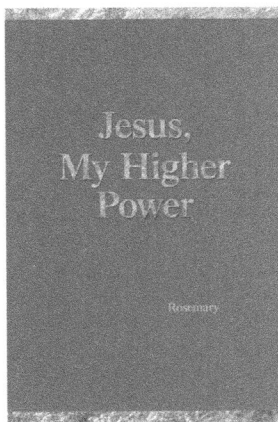

www.ingramcontent.com/pod-product-compliance
Lightning Source LLC
Chambersburg PA
CBHW030018290326
41934CB00005B/392